A DEFINED
REVELATION

FOR YE WHO QUESTION FAITH

JOSEPH LEWIS

LifeRich Publishing is a registered trademark of The Reader's Digest Association, Inc.

LifeRich Publishing books may be ordered through booksellers or by contacting:

LifeRich Publishing
1663 Liberty Drive
Bloomington, IN 47403
www.liferichpublishing.com
844-686-9607

Because of the dynamic nature of the Internet, any web addresses or links contained in this book may have changed since publication and may no longer be valid. The views expressed in this work are solely those of the author and do not necessarily reflect the views of the publisher, and the publisher hereby disclaims any responsibility for them.

Any people depicted in stock imagery provided by Getty Images are models, and such images are being used for illustrative purposes only. Certain stock imagery © Getty Images.

ISBN: 978-1-4897-3550-8 (sc)
ISBN: 978-1-4897-3549-2 (hc)
ISBN: 978-1-4897-3548-5 (e)

Library of Congress Control Number: 2021908186

Print information available on the last page.

LifeRich Publishing rev. date: 04/30/2021

CONTENTS

A PERSONAL INTRODUCTION

This collective work is material that has been honestly prayed for over the course of about two months. It was handwritten in a journal, transposed to an electronic medium, categorized by theme and intent, and then edited for structure and clarity. It is broken into five concise sections – each with a specific breadth of intellect, guidance, and fulfillment. These five sections have been placed in the order that they were written, but it is fair to note there is no real chronology necessary when confronting them – they are each independent of one another.

The first writing is a philosophical and theological affirmation free of any specific institutional religious belief system. It melds the topics of the conflicted mind, the origins of the mind, perceived truths of God, and how seeking these truths are fundamental to satisfying the purpose of the mind. There is only minor reference to actual philosophical critique provided since this work was not written by one who has any strong foundation in modern nor ancient philosophies. The theological stances are interwoven into the philosophical approaches mentioned simply by giving them reason or purpose.

The second writing displays an approach to Christianity that the writer believes to be a spiritual foundation for any person of faith, regardless of religious tendency. It discusses popular topics of sin, spiritual growth, and the implied significance of a man made God incarnate. For the modern Christian, it then recommends the importance of imitating Jesus throughout our lives and provides a path to do such.

The third writing details a reference to that which plagues our world and lives. A basic premise of demonology, the argument of good and evil, a religious chronological mapping of what has led us to today's iniquity, and the necessary tools to discourage evil and help live in accordance with God's will are all provided.

The fourth writing provides a personal interpretation of what love is and how we have become detracted from the essence of pure love. Love in society, love in the family, and love in the self are all topics briefly embraced.

The fifth writing gives insight into how judgment will be considered for any individual as well as some of the faults we may encounter within a lifetime. It does not depict fire nor brimstone but instead transposes the mentality necessary to prescribe oneself a satisfaction in occupation and spirituality.

Lastly, a few short poems were included to engage in a lyrical but direct approach of combining the various facets discussed throughout the whole work. It is a mere personal attempt to further bridge formations of thought and life.

May this small collection of writings grant you an internal peace, calling, or subjectivity to begin fashioning perceptions greater than what the senses have given you. While I would say it holistically addresses so much wrong in our world, it also addresses so much that is right. May you not be discouraged from realizing true potential and greatness in even the small aspects of life, for there in the dust and debris is where truth has been recorded.

A TESTIMONIAL TO CONVICTION

The Essentials

Philosophy is the basis for the human ability to justify reasoning. Theology is the philosophical approach towards connecting human perception with an eternal truth. Absolute Truth is unobtainable by humanity since Truth has existed prior to our existence and will persist after our existence. Divine Will always supersedes the human will and the Divine Mind always supersedes human reasoning. Mankind's will is governed by the Divine Will such that free will itself enables interaction between the two but the outcomes have already been planned through Divine Providence. Divine Providence is the preservation and enactment of the Divine Will. The utility of human reasoning resides in its precedence over physical occurrences such that the scope of our certainty lay confined to physicality.

Let that which relies on physical law focus on physicality, meaning anything confined to the senses. These were made by God, who is beyond physicality, but act as a medium through which both humans and God work. Physical law does not require divine intervention – its mechanism is already in motion. Physicality is far below God's presence; however, God will guide us when the mind and will are involved.

1

The Testimony

Blessed is the Divine Mind and the Divine Spirit.

The Conflicted Mind

A great sorrow grows when one believes wholeheartedly that his or her will and actions coincide with the Divine Will but discover that they have only forced God to look away. This sorrow is the conflicted mind. Living a life for one purpose – which is perceivably trying to fulfill God's will – but then internalizing that such an intended purpose had not abided by God's will is nothing short of ultimate betrayal and failure.

God's will appears to anyone with an agenda and conviction to pursue its enactment; however, because the Divine Will is being reasoned by humans, most likely it will not be fully perceived. Within our limited condition, we can attempt to use reasoning and free will to carry out the Divine Will respectably but never with certainty because the totality of God's will is unknown to humanity.

Another great sorrow grows when a loved one passes away. The bereavement of losing someone forces mixed emotions to swell. This is the sorrow of lost love. How can these feelings be quelled? The answer is acknowledgment of God's will not being beyond life or death, in any circumstance. Chance and coincidence do not mix with misfortune under Divine Providence. There are only physical bridges that have been carefully connected in order to yield specific outcomes.

The difference in these two sorrows is that the conflicted mind has no direct physical proof to work into its reasoning while the sorrow of lost love has a physical condition through which it can work. The conflicted mind is based on internalized perceptions that warrant action and purpose as well as warrant doubt. This yields a possible realization that the intended purpose may actually be outside of God's acceptance. The purpose – which was to seek God's favor – has been individually and mentally rejected despite original intent. Without a true physical conclusion to either rationalization – meaning acting in accordance with God or not – there is no true justification in either case. Both perceptions exist – one supported by purpose and a sense of fulfillment, the other hanging on by a thread of hope and faith.

A battle of right and wrong occurs daily in the human mind, one that varies in scale and clarity. It is a constant permeation of thought suffered by all regardless of discernment or reasoning but especially by those trying to fulfill the Divine Will. We are faced with an inherent reluctance that is often greater than our willingness to act.

This supports even more conflict – for no single person can advance the Divine Will alone, right? This is true. Advancing God's will through free will requires the actuality of God's favor and a blending of the two wills – alone nothing can be done. The key is understanding that our free will – although personally motivated – when running parallel with God's will is the exact necessity required to accomplish greatness in the world.

Upon having perceptions that one's own actions or even life do not coincide with God's will, a true sense of failure and betrayal manifests. This failure comes from having spent time in a seemingly futile effort; this betrayal comes from the inability to abide by God's will. These combine into a sorrow that casts the individual into a relative darkness where the mind searches for hope or reconciliation.

The mind must validate the good that was gained from such lost time as well as rationalize its own physical existence and purpose.

This in itself can be taxing on the mind as well as the will, leading to deep depression. The mind must also attempt to formulate ways to realign with God's will or seek redemption – two intangible goals that are difficult to achieve with certainty.

Thus, the mind is cast into a personal purgatory where it reflects on previous actions while trying to conceptualize future actions that will satisfy the following: its own physical purpose, what was learned from mistakes, a way to regain God's favor, and the will to do such – alone, inconclusive, and with no physical reassurance. This is truly the conflicted mind. One does not escape this mentality easily nor without first acknowledging the fallacies of such a mental state.

The Consolation

God's will cannot be overruled. This in itself would be sufficient for a conscientious and competent philosopher. Every attempt to fulfill God's will, whether perceived true or not, does exactly that. Free will is applied to our lives so that we may find peace and joy in understanding that our actions can help promote the inevitable advancement of the Divine Will; however, any and all actions were both completely necessary and also completely futile. This duality is beyond human reasoning but should provide comfort when acknowledged. No plausible effort in advancing God's will is done without some effect.

If reasoning that God's will cannot be overruled is insufficient, then perhaps recognizing that no person is ever alone in action or that no mind is ever without purpose will help pull one from this mental fall. The essential qualities of Godliness should support this reassurance, but first we must attempt understanding God. Humans are limited to physical laws; God is beyond physicality; thus, a limitless physical nature of God is apparent. This opposes notions of loneliness, for no one is ever alone – God is always there with us.

The mind is limited to human reasoning and emotion. Two-fold we fall short of the Divine Mind. Our personal reasoning allows for concepts to be misinterpreted, misunderstood, or irrationally justified – all of which are inconsistent with the Divine Mind. The Divine Mind has preordained Truth such that every time a human mind attempts to think or reason, that mind is merely attempting to strive for alignment with Truth.

There is no perceivable possibility that just because a human mind finds itself without purpose that this is actually true. It having been created in itself is enough to justify purpose and it is basically impossible for anyone to rationalize when its purpose has been fulfilled so long it continues to exist. Thus, the human mind can never truly justify it has no purpose if it continues to exist under the sovereignty of Divine Providence.

Emotions are personal and subjective but originate from common experience. The ages of humanity all seem to have a breath to them – a particular shared notion of what is acceptable to do and even how to think, perceive, and feel among others. Despite a shared collection of internalization, each person faces his or her own accumulation of emotion. Feeling emotion is a passionate motivation behind anyone's actions but it is common to attribute emotion solely to individual circumstance. God moves our emotions through the Divine Will and the simple act of feeling anything at all is a blessing in itself. Whether you are stricken with fear, sorrow, joy, or euphoria, it is done through allowances granted by the Divine Will.

No person feels any emotion alone – it is a shared experience with the Divine Spirit and holds purpose. Whether grief yields understanding or joy yields gratitude, there is a purpose behind each individual's emotions and timing. Therefore, when the human mind falls into true despair, it must make sense of the purpose behind such sorrow. The perpetual lessons of God may be hardening at times, but to a mind that cannot rationalize purpose behind emotion – whether perceivably good or perceivably bad – recovery from despair is difficult.

Once a mind can escape from innately experiencing emotions with disregard or impulse, and instead provide purpose to them, a large step can be made in the development of the self. If one can recognize that emotional sensation itself is beyond physicality, a journey towards God can begin. No person needs to be lost in his or herself for there are many faculties applied to humanity such as emotion which, with contemplation and focused thought, can lead to God, or back to God if it be forgotten.

The Purpose of the Mind

Understand that human thought is a medium constructed by the Divine Mind that allows free will as well as the exploration of Divine Providence. As a creature with no perceivable intellect, humans would be no different from animals; this is commonly accepted, especially since mankind's pride relishes in comprehending that it can comprehend at all. Regardless of everything a mind can know or remember, a daunting question persists – what is the purpose of the mind? Once we recognize the verity of our own intellectual potential, we can reasonably ask this question, for without internally acknowledging that the mind exists, the mind cannot question itself. Cognition and a perception of intellect is required.

Having been created prior to our own memory, there is a constant yearning for the mind to understand its origins. It asks itself, "from where did I come?" Parents satisfy a physical connection to the world but what satisfies the supernal relationship the mind shares with the world? We have an inherent desire for the mind to return to its own creation – another faculty of the mind that can lead one to God. The mind longs to seek God through wisdom and reason for once the mind can rationalize the futility of physicality, there is nowhere else to go but to the origin of the self.

Relative to each person, there was someone born prior to that person, and another who will die after that person. The expanse of time is not justified by our short duration of existence; thus, we individually seek to find peace in a seemingly tumultuous and overwhelming world. One can make the claim "time exists because I perceive it," but the opposite seems closer to truth – "I exist because it is my time." However, this arrangement cannot be satisfied without then wondering what the true beginnings were.

Satisfying the Purpose of the Mind

Philosophy is the first door one opens when wanting to seek more substance than what is physically provided. Physicality is not a means to find truth or wisdom – this task is performed by the mind. Also, physicality does not justify the mind's origins – only its existence. By building the foundation of a philosophical thought process, one can begin asking appropriate questions that, when answered, can truly bring a peace of mind. This peace of mind has the ability to consume and dissolve individual worries completely, but there are a few steps before this peace of mind can be obtained.

Quickly, I will state priority is in utmost humility and pure submission to God. At face value, these appear practical and obtainable, but when one realizes the intricacies of both, these two goals are fairly convoluted and require pure discipline of the body, mind, and spirit to develop.

7

I suppose it is here where I will state my intention and reason for writing as I do. It has always been a desire of mine to, with one simple dictation, impart the potential of the human mind to others and make a simpler path to God than the one that I have taken and am still on. As a man, it is sensible to leave behind that which makes life easier for others with similar inclinations. Without doubt, my life of sin and shame have led me to extraordinary vices and attempts of quelling pleasure and knowledge, but alas, nothing was fulfilling or completely satisfying until I was able to properly recognize the self and its connectivity to the world. Impulses, addictions, careless and reckless behaviors all led me, and I believe so many more, to a conditional surrounding built upon a foundation of pride and covered by falsity and fabricated self-control. Yet, even through this, whenever I reached a relative end, I felt gripped by something I did not understand, something that picked me up every time I let myself down. I mention utmost humility and pure submission to God not because I have heard about it or saw it in a pamphlet, but because it was truly the only way I could find any peace of mind validated by not just myself but also, seemingly, by a higher authority as well.

The most difficult part of being a human is understanding that you are something, and at the same time, you are nothing. Another duality that is rough to reason however I believe it holds true. By developing an utmost humility, you begin understanding just how insignificant you really are. Alone, you are unable to do most things and physically you are essentially dust in an endless world. With pure submission to God, you begin understanding exactly what value has been placed in you – an unbiased and impartial value brought upon you by Divine Providence. To the one who seeks truth, you will see how being nothing is everything to God.

THE PROCESS

Achieving Humility

Humility is a collection of specific characteristics as well as the conscious rejection of other characteristics. Primarily, being humble and showing humility involve being sensible, being aware of relations such as strengths and weaknesses, having humor, and understanding the utility of criticism. What humility does not involve are: pride, arrogance, anger, temper, nor seeking instant gratification. This general synopsis of humility is described with common human traits for easier consumption, but properly enacting a life of humility in any given situation requires much trial and error.

Acknowledge your faults, as well as other's faults, with patience. Understand no matter what strengths you behold, you are still just human. Maintain reasonable and obtainable expectations. And perhaps most importantly, realize the limitations of the human mind and the true fallacy of pride. These are a strong portion of the daily humble etiquette. Meanwhile, placing too much value on your strengths, exhibiting arrogance or boasting, acting impulsively or impatiently, and being unable to control your emotions are a strong portion of what is not enacting humility.

Socially exemplifying humility usually involves charity, volunteering, apprenticeships, and any act that puts others before yourself. Once you can value the time of others more than your own time, you begin finding a sense of peace and fulfillment nearly everywhere. Do not let the actions of others burden you. This is achieved in two ways – allow patience for other's unintentional shortcomings and do not become weighed down by another's intentional spite. Recognizing a person's fault is purely humbling when patience is applied. Recognizing deliberate fault in another and disallowing escalation is a good practice of emotional discipline.

These are mental and physical components of humility. With this shaping of the self, you will ultimately learn to enjoy life more fully as well as impart a gracious sense of compassion onto others constantly. The last act of humility applies to the spirit. Internally one must maintain a selfless and pious nature. This is the beginning of pure submission to God, the spiritual step to achieving peace of mind. Submission to God has been preached and taught in religious institutions and schools of thought for ages. Not only is seeking God the purpose of the mind but it is among the final life-changing steps that should be taken to promote fulfillment and happiness.

Submitting to God

Submission to God involves acknowledging the existence of God, seeking a relationship with God through the mind and spirit, physically acting in perceived accordance with God's will, and always placing God first when considering any action or thought. While humility assists in becoming selfless, submission to God fills the self with a redefined purpose and attitude.

Acknowledging the existence of God seems impractical to most because we build our perceptions based on the world around us, fixated on the self. Training the mind to maintain a scope that focuses on yourself – your life, your goals, your family, your wants – limits the potential of the mind. Without a foundation of thinking larger than self, larger than life, or larger than perception, there is little desire nor need to acknowledge God's existence.

Complacency, self-satisfaction, and a narrow mind offer exactly what a human *wants* in life. I argue that getting exactly what you want is unfulfilling, not because it doesn't bring about satisfaction but because it doesn't unfold the full spectrum of life. Fulfillment is a deep feeling of satisfaction, gratitude, and accomplishment; it satisfies the spirit, not just the body or mind. Learning new ideas, sciences, and theorems is a great mental feeling, and living with physical aptitude is renewing to the body, but where does the spirit get its fill? An inherent yearning for God exists in each person, implanted upon birth and awaiting its journey through life. It is the breath of spirit placed in each of us.

Another Ontological Argument

God's existence can be justified by many ways. Here, I will describe how to rationalize God through philosophy, meaning through reasoning, as well as how to rationalize God through introspection, a meditative practice of comparing the relationship of the self, the mind, and the universe as it is perceived.

An initial step to justifying any one thing's existence is being able to imagine it within the mind. Without a mental image of the object meant to be reasoned, the mind would fail in the process of rationalization. Therefore, imagine what characteristics of God would seem appropriate to shaping an initial image of God. Characteristics, qualities, traits – anything we typically associate with an intellectual being such as ourselves. This mental portrait of God will be limited by one's own capability of melding all the qualities together, for as our perception becomes overwhelmed, we begin remembering qualities left out or forgetting essential ones.

The purpose is to imagine that there could perceivably exist a being whose qualities and characteristics supersede those of any other being. The whole omnipotence, omniscient, overly just, and kind "template" sticks with most people's initial view, but recognize that even this is just a portion of the whole. Consider always being true, just, benevolent, forgiving, merciful, gracious, powerful, generous, and above all, eternal. The reality is such a conceptually perfect being is beyond human perception, but we can attempt to come close by essentially creating a melting pot of every possible virtuous trait we can recall. This should yield a basis for what we believe God to be – something that knows everything, can do anything, all the time.

With the semblance of a mental image of God, next we need a purpose for God because it is more rational to deduce – purpose warrants existence. Nothing truly exists without function or a role to play. Therefore, imagine what purpose God could possibly have. What role could God possess among others? Being a creator? Being a teacher? Being a tyrant? Being a thing that doesn't need purpose to exist except merely to exist? If the role is plausible, then it can rationally hold as an argument, regardless of truth.

A perceived purpose combined with a mental perception of God reasonably satisfies existence to the philosopher. Empirically, this formula would not satisfy existence because one cannot interact or use sensual analysis of God. However, and let my bias against empiricists be known, I argue these two concepts formed from the mind are more than enough to satisfy existence; here is my stance: traits associated with God, such as omnipresence, easily suggest being unconstrained by physicality, such that it is irrational to reduce the existence in question to the limitations of the interpreter or philosopher. What empirical data could possibly be derived from our finite senses when considering an existence beyond physicality? Our constraint to physicality does not grant authority to reason that if an existence beyond physicality exists, it too must be constrained to physicality. Our minds and thoughts supersede physicality, do they not exist?

Following these two steps, we have created enough individual satisfaction to reason the existence of God. To many, this won't substantiate the necessity of God, meaning that even if such a being exists, what use is there to believe in it? In other words, what true reason does one have for justifying God's existence? We now have two concepts: justifying the existence of God (done) but also justifying the need to justify the existence of God. This will begin the introspection portion of clarifying not just God's existence but why striving to reason it is beneficial to the individual. The philosophical portion was simple to ascertain because truth, usually, comes from simplicity. That always seems most reasonable.

Introspective Meditation

Introspection, meaning to form a deep perception of one's own self and its relationship with the universe, is subjective, but the method in which one can perform introspection is fairly universal. Maintaining the basis that the mind and spirit yearn for union with God can help guide one's thoughts more easily during introspection. If one prefers to reject the existence of God and still perform introspection, I will place two road maps and, hopefully, for even this work is dynamic, we will arrive at the same result.

Relinquishing Physicality

Introspection performed without regard to the existence of God originates in the self, naturally. Ask yourself questions that are important to you regarding the nature of things. What comes to mind when considering the nature of things? Life? The weather? Societies and governments? Crashing waves on a desolate island? How should you raise your children? Each of us has such an array of specific interests and concerns that any mind inquiring about the nature of things will never be the same, person to person.

However, take that which you find most significant to ponder and apply an unbiased approach to finding your relationship to it all, an approach that would allow for anyone to have a similar impartiality. For instance, consider all physical possession in life is relinquished – your house, money, clothes, jewelry, cars. These physical attachments act as obstacles to the mind when trying to find oneself. Physical objects created by humans or given value by humans inherently have a lesser value than anything derived from the mind. If they are lesser, how do they act as obstacles? They are physical necessities in one's usual state of being that the mind must rationalize. This hinders mental advancement. If physical possession is unable to be overlooked, then an apparent mental obstacle is already in place before beginning, preventing the mind from functioning more fully.

Until you understand the futility in these obstacles – physical attachment, physical desire, pride, and physical reputation – it is difficult to continue with introspection. Physical attachment is the physical necessity of things you have, physical desire is the physical necessity of things you want, pride is the persistent reasoning that everything you have experienced or rationalized until now is Truth itself, and physical reputation is the value of your physical image based on physical expectation. A common reason humans find letting go of physicality difficult is due to pride and fear – pride in letting go of what has been "earned" and fear of what he or she would be without anything enhancing his or her image.

Upon giving up physical attachment to objects, what remains? To a family, just that – each other. If you are single – yourself. How does this compare to animals? Notice how stripping physical attachment from animals does not really affect them – physicality is there entire nature. Animals are perceivably of a lower order than humans, not because they have no value, but because they have difficulty with reasoning, morality, and acting on anything but instinct. Yet when we strip ourselves of physical attachment, we ultimately find ourselves physically matched by animals. Without physical attachment, humans revert to a simpler identity within nature. Despite the world in which we grew up and matured, we have a perceptive ability to see ourselves without any of it – no racism, no elitism, no hatred, no systemic rule, no immediate demand for wealth. Without physical desire, we are all naturally equal.

With physical attachment removed, we strive to have a clearer and more impartial view of the world around us. It also lets the next step seem easier. We currently have a scene where there is no physical necessity, meaning no attachment to physical objects. The next step is removing the physical need of the body. Complete physical detachment is the removal of the self from physicality – meaning letting the mind attempt to reach its full potential without any need for physicality – a difficult but necessary step to take.

When physicality itself is removed, what remains of you? An empty shell? Do you not think? Ideals? Hopes? Can you now see? Without physicality, it is clearer why the senses are lesser than the mind – for all that remains is your mind wondering "what is going on?"

Compare our mental situation to that of animals. Aren't we inherently more supreme than them intellectually? An animal is unable to fully remove itself from physicality because that is exactly what its natural identity is, whereas we as humans can utilize reason, intellect, and perception to separate ourselves from that which is purely physical. Animals rely on instinct to live; humans are not forced to solely rely on such.

The Self

This capability of separating from physicality, if only mental, permits a state of mind many do not utilize. You must remove yourself through detachment before looking within and seeing yourself fully. Perceiving yourself without being hindered by physical necessity also allows you to see the futility in physicality itself. If you separate yourself by detachment, who can honestly claim that you no longer have value or purpose? The mind itself is enough of a personal manifestation to warrant value – the mind supersedes physicality; therefore, even without physicality, you exist within the limitations of your perception. This is essentially the *true* you – the complete accumulation of memory, experience, beliefs, personal truths – all free from physical necessity. The mind does not require natural law to exist, but it uses physicality as a means of expression and embodiment.

Pondering the Creation of the Mind

Now the humbling and perhaps intricate part of introspection occurs. Can you rationalize that you created your own mind or that you acted as a component in its creation? Can you attribute any physical occurrence to its creation? How can the mind rationalize its own creation if it cannot justify having created itself? How could anyone claim to have created his or her own mind? Is it so absurd to imagine the mind's creation – due to it being beyond physicality – is also beyond physical means? This simple idea seems more reasonable than suggesting the faculties of the mind were created purely by some existent physical process.

The difficulty for us at this point is feasibly understanding how to rationalize the mind's origin and creation. Looking at physicality will never bring a satisfactory answer, and being removed from physicality, we are just left in limbo, perceivably in our own mind that we are trying to rationalize. Where can one go? The human mind itself is limited, but it is capable of rationalizing concepts easily as long as a reasonable path has been created to connect points of reason – meaning perceivably conclusive ideals.

Truth to the mind is anything that satisfies its own criteria, and perception helps view what is true to the mind itself. A perceivable truth exists for each of us – it is the accumulation of all rationalized perceptions previously experienced.

Before venturing on a path to the mind's creation, let us see the relationship between perceived truth and pride. Perceived truth is a faculty of the mind that remembers all previously rationalized perceptions and acts as a filter for any future perceptions. Pride is the affirmative stance that this perceived truth is in actuality Truth itself.

What is the relationship between perceived truth and Absolute Truth? Truth itself has and always will supersede any perceived truth; however, at times they will run parallel to one another and yield appropriate reasoning. There is no reasonable way for humanity to obtain Absolute Truth without Truth revealing itself. Using appropriate deduction can yield a perceived truth sufficient to the individual, and with discipline can more effectively correlate to Truth.

What is left to accomplish in introspection? We have a mind removed from physicality contemplating its own origins without actually having the means to rationalize anything with complete certainty, only a possible conclusion that satisfies a perceivable truth. In essence, we have to convince ourselves with a good enough perception so that we can reasonably internalize it. Individuality will render various points of reason that lead to a perceivable truth, but I will present one meditation that can ultimately lead the mind to its own creation while satisfying requirements of a perceived truth.

Meditating on the Self

Traversing one's own mind can be quite tedious but revealing. Validating the mind's creation, existence, and purpose requires some backtracking, as if mental breadcrumbs have been left for us, and to follow them we will need to meditate.

Imagine a scenery or location that is pleasing to you. The more detail you add to it, the more demand required to recall it, so try to keep it realistic but readily accessible. In this mental scene, also place yourself experiencing fair emotion – meaning peace, joy, or maybe excitement. You would never want to have emotions such as fear, anger, or sorrow present. For me, I imagine myself in the middle of a pond, sitting, floating right on the water, and it is calm. Whichever scenario you have constructed exists in the mind – refine it and remember it.

Meditate on this scene and try to perceive yourself experiencing whichever emotions bring you peace. For my pond, the calm serenity allows for a break from stress or demand. Even if I ripple the water it brings me joy. As the seasons change, I enjoy the imagined landscape. Does watching the meditated you calm you down and bring peace? The goal is to find a relative peace, even a small piece of peace, within the mental fabrication of your own self-image. You want to see the *mental* you just as happy as you want the *physical* you to be.

Now perceive the relationship between the physical you and the mental you. How are they connected? Does the physical you exist and within its own vessel, seemingly the head, the mental you exist? Or does the mental you exist and simply gain physical form through natural laws? In some ways, aren't both of these stances true? Both are the same *you* just with different relative expression.

The physical you exists within physical limitations and within its mental construct exists a thought given the form of a mentally perceived you. But also, the mental image of yourself now exists – the you who is at peace – and to the best of its ability is trying to manifest through the physical you. It's almost like looking into a mental or dimensional mirror of the self. Mind supersedes physicality almost as if it were a higher dimension.

A Conclusive Claim

Where does connecting the physical you and the mental you leave us? Well, now we have two different existing images of the same you, simultaneous and parallel. Which of these did you create? The mental image is a product of the mind – meaning mental faculties available to you were used to create the mental perception of yourself.

You create all recollections of the mind for yourself, but can you remember creating your own mind? These mental faculties existed upon your own existence, so there is no rational way to have done such. However, you clearly needed the mind itself to create this mental image. How could you ever have created a mind for yourself without already having had a mind?

Physically we were created through usual means, and this can be observed, recorded, and proven because we are able to work through natural law by natural law. But we have already reasoned that physicality is lesser than mentality; therefore, the governing laws of physicality should, too, be lesser than the governing laws of the mind.

We return to the question, "how was my mind created?" Now we have some mental breadcrumbs to lead the way – the mind was not created by physical means, for physicality is less than that of the mind, but we can reason that the mind can create within itself, just as we have done, and if the mind cannot rationalize it created itself, then there must be another mind responsible for its creation. Nothing can be created without a mind or some faculty resembling our perception of what a mind is.

Now the final step in this mental journey – we return to that scenery where the you with genuine peace exists. That scene exists in your mind, created by your own mind. If we follow this similar causal relationship of creation, then our minds, too, exist within the Divine Mind that created them. Try to meditate on that.

There exists something beyond physicality responsible for creating that which is greater than physicality and has connected the means of the mind with the means of physicality such that both exist within perceivable limitations.

Natural order such as weather, orbits, migratory patterns and changing tides are all governed by natural laws that yield to efficiency. Such is true for philosophical tendencies – meaning processes of the mind – except efficiency is replaced by reason. As we try reasoning that which is physically present, we are constantly relying on a resource provided to us and not originally from ourselves – our own minds. And if our minds exist within another, I would argue that everything we perceive does as well, just as our self-image exists within our own mind.

A New Purpose

This claim returns us to the original goal of seeking humility and a foundation on which to build our self. By being unable to rationalize that we played a role in the creation of our own minds, we have a chance to recognize a true component of creation existing beyond our perception – for which we ought to be thankful. More importantly, we ought to be humbled by the specific circumstance that allowed our being existent at all.

Who can truly say his or her own existence carries significant value? Imagine the error each individual performs – all the anger, dread, sorrow, or pain inflicted by other's actions. Others suffer constantly because of another's existence; yet, despite this seeming unfairness, we continue to exist. Why? Only Truth knows for certain, and the longer we stray from seeking that truth, more suffering will be endured.

Where does humanity have to go other than re-recognizing itself? The simplest and most accessible attribute of ourselves is the mind, and we can't even find reason for its creation nor give credit where credit is due. We attempt to claim an inherent right to even exist, but we don't have the authority to make such a claim. What rightfully satisfies natural order keeping mankind intact other than simply trying to fix its own mistake?

Or perhaps, there is an inherent value placed in each of us and as a whole. One that is not fully understood but has been or will be revealed. What is the value of a life? We strive for advancement, growth, gaining knowledge, gaining physical objects, but what is an almost instinctual response when confronted with another who is in trouble? We are willing to give any of that up to effectively cease the suffering of another, sometimes even paying with our own life. Imagine truly what you would do for a loved one in need; what would you do to save the life of your own child? The value of a life is represented in its ability to be given, not in its effectual reception of *things*.

What does it mean to give one's life? Death doesn't have to be the perpetual answer. Utilizing the characteristics of humility and charity allow for a fulfillment and repaying of the value of life itself. Just as we are willing to sacrifice time and attention for a loved one, we must attempt being respectful and grateful for existing at all. We have traversed the mind not only to find ourselves, but to find a glimpse of what truth may actually be. I can say with certainty I am not responsible for the mere concept of existing at all. Who could? We must fill ourselves with a gratitude, a humbling, true, unhindered, and unblinded gratitude for that which allows anything to be at all.

It is human folly and pride that clouds reasonable judgment on the nature of things. We prescribe ourselves just enough self-worth to permit any wrongdoing, become apathetic to punishment, and inoculate ourselves with faculties of the mind that justify our own superiority despite having had no role in the creation of such faculties of the mind. The truth behind Truth is that no person can obtain it in its fullness – it has predated us, and it will outlive us. This in itself should be humbling to any creature of intellect because with the remnants of a forgotten truth, we continue to exist. It is natural to ponder large questions such as creation and purpose, but the answers to these questions were provided long ago such that by even continuing to exist should be enough justification of purpose.

And ultimately, this is utmost humility – accepting that our individual perceived truths are at best a piece of Truth itself, and we can never with certainty attribute ourselves to our own creation, but it has been willed by something greater than us, and from that we find gratitude. This is the best foundation on which to build oneself, for admitting one's own ignorance is not blind faith but the closest to truth one can reasonably obtain.

A Way to Grow

Similar to talking to the self in the mind when reasoning internally, an internal and personal dialogue ought to be pursued relating belief, intentions, and concerns with the Divine Mind. Just as you internalize your own words in silence, you can internalize a personal connection and relationship with the perceived Creator. To most, it may seem odd to talk to yourself but let me implore you to find sanctuary within your mind so that you can release troubled thoughts.

If we remember the self-image created in the mind, we can see creations seem to get stuck in the mind – they don't manifest physically without direct action. The mind begets the mind. Your personal representation of yourself at peace exists in the Divine Mind. It is already a personal connection made through supposedly unknown mental faculties but are made very apparent when you full-heartedly reach out with your vocal mind to release doubts, concerns, or adoration of what life has been for you.

The Divine Mind hears and welcomes a personal conversation, no matter how silly it may be. To anyone attuned to the ideology of spirits and angels, understand within your mind you are safe – there is sanctity in the temple of the mind when it is fortified with utmost humility, submission to God, and the fullness of your spirit.

Religious institutions teach prayer as a means for communicating with God. This meditative practice of completely directing spiritual focus on an internalized conversation and plea towards God can be even more effective.

When a pure sense of devotion and spiritual commitment emits from yourself, you will notice a change in your life. You will undoubtedly begin a meaningful and eternal relationship with your Creator, God, the Divine Mind, and the fulfillment of all.

A Closing

I hope skeptics still questioning God's existence can reasonably justify or consider that a Divine Mind is an acceptable rationalization. Certainty of Truth can never be granted until we outwardly and internally seek it – may you find footing on the path leading back to origins. My inclination is to have a universal blend of philosophical and theological tendencies such that any one person can find a comfort or sense of purpose in life.

It is simply beyond me personally not to emphasize the state of mind in which we currently are. I speak through written word to summarize the previous perceptions placed before us into a compact memory – although truth is beyond full comprehension, do not be discouraged when life seems unfair, for it is only out of focus. Detach from physicality and find yourself within yourself. When you see the fragile you within you, fully reach out with the vocal mind. The faculties of the mind will guide you through any situation and compose your spirit along the way. This is all beyond full comprehension but with utmost humility and submission to the unknown truth called God, anyone can be pulled back into the light of life.

Remember that an internal dialogue is essential for submission to God. A binding relationship allows for the growth of the self, mind, and spirit, while also presenting praise and gratitude towards God. Do not be deterred from conventional prayer, meditation, or simply consciously thinking about God as you travel the world, thinking of the purpose of it all. Once the mind and spirit have become strengthened with a bit of zeal, you will be able to physically conduct yourself more properly. Living according to God's will means trusting in Him completely as well as asking for guidance through life.

We have found ourselves within the Divine Mind; now we must allow others to perceive truth for themselves. I strongly believe the Divine Spirit works through all of us, whether we know it or not. To those unaware, I hope this simple meditative and philosophical journey has allowed you to open a door to simple truth. Right or wrong, I cannot deny establishing a perceived truth committed fully to humility and God is nothing but a step in the right direction.

Whatever is left to be in this work, I do not know, but I feel compelled to make this section final such that...

In all Divine Grace and Divine Mercy, I hope peace and happiness can fill your vessel of life.

A CHRISTIAN PLEA

A Joyous Rant

What greater sense of love could exist for a person than that of knowing one's own complete and unhindered devotion, loyalty, and submission to God is being received? To those of faith and hope, let the spirit of virtue and fear of the Lord fill you with the fullest humility such that you cannot help but kneel and pray to God.

How great is God when we realize the simple natures of ourselves – shamed by sin, covered in lies, reluctant to testify or acknowledge God's blessings – and yet, despite this personal reality, His reality is so great that even our disharmony can be shown mercy and grace. How eternally great is He who can turn hearts of the wicked and utterly destroy the temptation of Earthly pleasures and desires? How great is He who can eliminate all material want and replace it with charity?

As He has given endlessly, we ought to give continuously. The sun does not cease to shine when we need it to light our way – a perfect representation of unconditional sacrifice – for neither does the mercy and love of our God. Embrace it and welcome it into your body, mind, and soul because it is the only certainty of greatness one can experience here in a temporal realm.

A Less Joyous Rant

It's a hard life to live, one in which the existence of God is denied. How do so many of us even survive such a difficult life? Why do so many of us choose to live such an impossible life? We feed ourselves after minor victories and disregard our major defeats, whether physical, educational, relational, or even just from self-reflection. Do you believe you can advance yourself on your own? Does your pride not even let you see your own prideful self? Blind in regards to the reality of the world around you, blind to the reality of your own circumstance, and blind to the resources available to assist and guide you – why would one choose this way of living?

It would be to your benefit to deny yourself just a moment of pride and submit to the natural humility within you. Break down if that's what you need to call it, but by any means necessary find a way to see yourself for what and who you really are. You don't have to live blindly behind the veil of deceit that congratulates self-honor and self-worth while devaluing the connections outside yourself. Take a step back and enjoy the perspective from outside yourself, for just a moment. The families, the households, the animals, the strife, the ambitions, the failures, the people. Enjoy them. Here and now. For they won't all be there in the end.

The Beginning of Spirit

Upon being baptized, the soul begins its transformation. What was once the body of the Earth and flesh has now become a proper vessel in which the Holy Spirit may work. What once was a spirit or soul hindered by sin and human nature has become an active and fertile vineyard where seeds of proper virtue and wisdom can be grown. Without an initial baptism, we are constrained to the deficiencies of human nature including pride in knowledge, apathy towards punishment and repercussion, and a self-proclaimed sovereignty over other men.

The Importance of the Ascension

Original sin is the exact representation of disharmony and the falling from grace that has yielded the human condition in which we live. The seemingly simple act of eating a fruit may cause many to second guess the true justice of God however this act, in its principal, was a direct violation of the only price of eternal grace and favor – to not disobey God. Therefore, into our current condition each of us has been born, unknowingly, already inflicted with the treacherous sin that ruins our communion and connection to the Holy Spirit and God.

The children of Adam – meaning the generations proceeding Adam – had to bear the sins of their generations until the point in time where sin was too prevalent among themselves. Thus, the first baptism of humanity occurred – the Flood. God preserved enough of the lineage of Adam to allow for reconciliation in the future, which would not take place until Christ's coming from the womb of the Blessed Virgin Mary.

Prior to Christ's ascension, baptism of the soul allowed that soul to wait for this aforementioned ascension upon death. Once the embodiment of God ascended to Heaven, an important piece of the puzzle for salvation and rectifying sin was fulfilled.

The Immaculate Conception of Mary

To give more example of how Original sin affects humanity, we can expand on the Immaculate Conception of Mary – whom God chose as the holy vessel to birth his own Son, a man who would encapsulate the immensity of God Himself.

Mary was not born through regular means such as other humans; the direct implanting of God's full grace was placed in the womb of her righteous and pious mother – Saint Anne – whom swore to chastity and was unable to bear children. God gave her the promise of a child through his Angelic messengers, and in the later stages of her life Saint Anne and her husband Joachim conceived a child by the will of God. Saint Anne gave birth to Mary free from pain, for Mary was not born with original sin but instead with a connectivity to God and His heavenly host of Angels – a most suitable and perfect embodiment for the Mother of God.

Being free from original sin, Mary was able to live a life full of utmost virtue, humility, and piety as well as remain free from regular temptations of this realm. Her perfect purity was meant to represent the Eve who had not sinned and was achieved through being born of God's grace, whereas Eve was born of Adam. In essence, Mary has been the only person to ever walk the Earth without the implied suffering of humanity due to sin. Even Jesus was able to be tempted by the devil whereas Mary was impervious to temptation.

The Reality of Sin

The belief of how each of us is affected by original sin is naturally paramount to the Christian faith, but don't be mistaken, the truths of sin are abundant in any faith. Being born into this chaotic and temporal realm in itself is an initiation into a lifelong journey of trying to find oneself through obtaining wisdom, discovering the faculties of the mind, achieving internal peace, becoming a compassionate and loyal member of society, and fulfilling a relationship with God.

Regardless of the theological channels with which you are familiar, it is presumed that we are not born perfect nor without purpose. This commonality of belief is the beginning of uniting the faiths of the world. One cannot deny that the essential elements of religion and underlying truths are present in all religious and theological documentation. We all have our doctrines detailing specific lives of enlightened and holy men and women, the paths taken to obtain wisdom, and what it means to have a body, mind, and soul.

Coincidentally, we as humans have basic principles and reasoning relevant to life, ethics, morality, health, relationships, and family. Any contradiction to these understood and innate values of common good is the result of that chaos into which we are all born. The malice, the envy, the greed, the direct negligence of peace – these are all products of our original sin. We wear shame and dishonor daily, not by our own choosing or our own actions, but by an inherited sin that we cannot avoid, and when we develop a disdain or misunderstanding of why this is our human condition, the resultant emotions and negativity are what drive us to suffering.

The Plea

Please, I humbly beg, walk with me through one religious account of how to remove yourself from the sin that plagues our inherent human nature and, in its place, find grace and peace in God. Whether we believe ourselves to be good people in general, without grace, pure perfection is unobtainable by humanity – for this quality is reserved for God's presence alone. The only account of religious doctrine recording this specific presence of God is in Christianity for Jesus Christ himself was the embodiment of God.

No other person can attest to this claim in any other teaching. Whether your personal beliefs support or deny this claim, I ask you to keep an open mind and heart to ponder how such a belief exists in the world, for the existence of Jesus is universally accepted, deeming him at least to be a righteous man who walked the path to God.

If the question is how can such a man exist, then what follows is the rational theological and spiritual answer. Recalling the Immaculate Conception of Mary – Jesus' mother – her birth was preordained by God such that she would be entrusted with the fullness of the grace of God. This allowed Mary to be born free from sin, which would reasonably be the only acceptable womb from which God's Divinity could come into this world.

God Himself dispatched at least 1000 Angels of the highest order to watch over Mary from the immaculate conception itself and throughout her entire life, whereas typically any individual receives but one Angel and of any order. As Mary grew in age, so did her mental faculties that kept her close to God and helped her abide by His will entirely, so much so that when the time came to announce she would bring the Son of God into the world she knew no other answer than "let it be."

We now have the perfect formula through which the Holy Spirit could work its miracle – the womb of a woman who has been free of sin by God's will in a woman who has devoted the entirety of her life to God's will giving permission to allow for the virgin birth of the Son of God just as God wills. Nothing is greater than God's will, and in this account, which is the very inception of Christianity itself, we have God willing that He come among humans in the flesh.

If this may be contradictory to your own beliefs, at least attempt to reason that in order for God to come in the flesh, He would require specific circumstances that would allow the world to behold his immense divinity itself. Such circumstance is perceivably having a woman full of grace, free of sin, and a virgin birth – for the furthest from man a woman could be is the closest to God she could ever be. This is a theological answer of how such a man could exist, for he beheld the nature of man, but also the divine nature of God Himself.

From this point on, the true Christian message will be dictated. If you have a soul to save, may God will that you continue.

The Christian Calling

Do not let the rupture of mankind's prideful and zealous fervor disallow your chance to truly become free of sin and begin anew spiritually. No matter what faith and belief we hold in our hearts, if the prime focus is on peace for humanity and acting in accordance to God's will, then the one true God is being glorified.

Our constant conflict of deciding who is right or wrong is an exact product of original sin; it is not a divine or holy order from God – it is a manmade perception created out of our own incestuous and confused sin. Do not become a victim of this sensually chaotic world.

By whatever faculty of faith or reasoning you can muster in your heart and mind, take one leap of faith and pursue baptism in the name of the Holy Father. To all brothers and sisters of faith, I claim the cost may be too high not to do such. Validate within yourselves a reason to cease the burdens and ties of sin. Pray, meditate, and contemplate on what the simple act of Baptism could do for your soul. Maintain practicing your faith as you see fit in order to praise and glorify God, but please do not immediately reject the perceivable benefit of being baptized just like a long-lost brother of faith – one whom we cannot deny walked on the path toward God – Jesus Christ.

Spiritual Growth

Baptism is the first step into a spiritual life supported by the Holy Spirit itself. The physical body is born of the womb whereas the spiritual body is born of the sacrament of baptism – a full natured spirituality would not exist without such an act.

What does one do with a newly applied spirituality? Honestly, nearly nothing except allow the Holy Spirit work with you. Your true spiritual journey will take more time than you are given within a life; however, when you become receptive to its workings, a sense of wisdom, comfort, and fulfillment will come about.

To hasten the efficacy of a spiritual transformation, I will present a fundamentally trying path to walk following baptism. As a Christian, we develop a desire to understand Christ as well as what has really occurred in our history and how it affects us today. How can we be good Christians?

Remember the fall of Adam and Eve bore original sin on humanity, not because of anything we have currently done, but because the sins of humanity persist through lineage. Preceding generations had to live in sin until wiped away by the Flood. This flood opened an era for humans to repopulate the world until the time was right for God to become man and, once again, rid the world of sin by His own sacrificial offering of Jesus.

Prior to the ascension of Jesus, it was impossible to have been Christian; yet we still carry the sinful lineage from the times before Christ as a humanity. This is such a profound spiritual dilemma because until one becomes baptized, that individual would just be living in pure sin regardless of action, morality, or mentality. We had a direct intervention from God that allowed for repentance and reconciliation in what was otherwise a seemingly perpetual sinful human nature. By God's mercy, we were allowed a chance to regain God's grace by believing in Christ's sacrifice and receive renewal of the spiritual nature of humanity through baptism and living a Christ-like life.

Living Like Christ

But what is a Christ-like life? Referring to exactly what happened to Jesus allows us to correlate and connect specific occurrences overlapping in the life of Christ and in our own lives. There are primary stages of Christ's life and why it is important to recognize them is this – Christ, having been born with the divine nature of God Himself through the womb of the Blessed Virgin Mary makes him the only man to uphold the exact nature and path required to conquer the sin of the world. Christ's life was not just an act of God's mercy but also a direct reflection on our own lives and how humanity should develop within its sinful state.

Vocation

First, we live a life of vocation – one that attaches us to the world and establishes our role in it. Being born of the world means you are connected to it and will have to make a living and grow as humans of your time do. What do we have today? Education, work, and retirement. It is a neat little package ingrained into our focus, but this will not satisfy the spiritual growth of anyone.

When one tires of this perpetual mold of human life, and recognizes the value of mind and spirit, true grace and mercy can be found. Christ worked as a carpenter until he was compelled to follow tradition and become baptized. This is the case with many people today who may not have grown up in a religious household and have found religion later in life – myself included.

Baptism

Then, upon baptism, we begin to develop our own spirituality internally. Note how Jesus did not begin to teach until after His baptism. Though Jesus Himself was the embodiment of God, He was still subjected to human nature in its lowly form. The effective working of the Holy Spirit became instilled in Jesus upon baptism.

Temptation

Upon His baptism and the beginnings of the Holy Spirit working through him, the devil tries tempting Jesus – for once the foundation of one's own spirit is formed, true temptation can become more apparent. Prior to baptism, we already live in sin; there is no need for us to recognize temptation. Following baptism, original sin is removed and thus the devil and the other fallen angels must try to reclaim that person through sin and tempting to sin. Because Jesus beheld a divine nature, His faculties and discretion were much keener than our own such that He could negate temptation and truly begin a life of devotion and loyalty to God's will.

I believe this is the stage most Christians reach in their lifetime before succumbing to temptation or believing that a permanent sanctifying grace exists in his or her own baptism. However, this is not the case. Baptism removes original sin and only begins the next chapter in one's spiritual life as a Christian.

We as humans are not sinless creatures and tend to sin quite often – even small acts of displeasure to God. Without the sacrament of confession, an absolving of sin committed after baptism cannot occur. Prayer of contrition and confession are required to live free of sin; thus, Christians have their itinerary and manner in which to live life, and opposed to this, the devil and his fallen angels also have to maintain their own course of action to divert any inclinations or actions to live sin free.

It is an unfortunate reality for most Christians to face because, and I believe it to be the regular deception and complacency in the world, we believe baptism and the belief in Christ is enough to sanctify and save a soul. Without regular mass – to forgive venial sin – and confession – to forgive mortal sin – many of us are living a prideful and sinful life, believing we have done enough to be saved already. Hence the reality of living a true Christ-like life does not just stop after baptism nor overcoming temptation – it continues.

Wisdom and Virtue

Following the baptism and temptation, Christ was led to live and act in accordance with God's will and enact His true purpose as the Son of God. Christians striving to live like Christ might dilute life's journey to simply upholding the Commandments of God, and while this is important, it is relatively difficult to do without failing from time to time.

True wisdom and virtue are not supplied by baptism – we just become more receptive to the Holy Spirit's teachings. The tribulations of life and strict studying of scripture and religious texts promote a virtuous and holy life, hence this portion of Christ's life – abiding by the will of God. Because you are baptized and believe in Christ does not excuse nor pardon you from continuing to develop your spirit and living like Christ. Just as Jesus taught, preached, and performed generous acts, we too must strive for this individually. You were baptized but do you know scripture? Do you understand theology? Do you understand why the world is in such a condition as it is?

It is pivotal for the salvation of a soul to delve into the minds and spirits of those who came before us – holy men and women, saints, teachers, and members of the Church. Otherwise, our complacent minds will likely fall into a great pride and falling away from God. The knowledge, wisdom, and virtues of life were inherent in Christ, but for any Christian to live like Christ, these must be obtained through study, work, acts of generosity, and prayer.

Persecution

This leads us to the last two portions of Jesus' life – the persecution and crucifixion – without doubt, the hardest part of Christ's life to fully practice as a Christian. The persecution comes from enacting a will that doesn't match the expectation of an area, usually due to religious conflict or disagreement. Preaching and teaching in the name of Jesus is the exact purpose of persecution.

Most of us live a life and have a vocation completely outside of the Church, such that the idea of preaching regularly is unthinkable. I simply say try to welcome at least one individual into the belief of Christ within your lifetime. This is most easily done through marriage, but really strive to introduce the sanctity of Christ to anyone. Save a soul as well as protect your own. For persecution in its harshest forms do not come upon all of us, but remember, to many it did. Life and blood have been spilled just as Christ's had.

Crucifixion

This points us towards the final part of Christ's physical life – the crucifixion – the ultimate sacrifice for humanity and the final enactment of God's will. How can Christians become crucified daily? Practices such as Lent add a means of suffering to the lives of Christians but to expand on this would be performing regular acts of mortification.

Mortification of the soul is anything that subjects one to humility and reasonable suffering. Giving up vices, giving up pleasures, fasting regularly, incessant prayer, or anything personal to an individual such as cold showers, flagellation, or physical exertion are all examples of mortification.

The crucifixion of Christ was brutal and difficult to imitate in a symbolic nature, but to carry out the rest of our days comfortably and complacently is definitely not the way to live or die like Christ. Whatever acts of mortification you perform, remember to have the sacrifice of Christ in mind and in your heart. Acknowledge that nothing you can really do to mortify yourself can come close to what really happened in Golgotha – this will also subject you to utmost humility, knowing that even your own suffering is never good enough.

Understanding Sin

The crucifixion of Christ dawned a new age of humanity. Prior to the crucifixion, Christianity did not exist, the church today did not stand; it all began with the final and purest sacrifice given to the previous age of humanity – Jesus Himself, the sacrificial lamb of God. The age of Adam was meant to be lived in a particular way such that humanity would uphold God's commandments through obedience and also offer sacrifice. Sin needed to be confronted in that sinful age in completely different means than the age following the crucifixion of Christ.

For one to comprehend what sin even is, imagine it as such – this created realm in which we live has a harmonious and flowing resonance to it; when everything is done according to God's law and will, it plays ceaselessly and perfectly. But as soon as sin – that being the opposition of God's law or will – is committed, a harsh and dissonant vibration of existence is released, one that cannot be undone except by specific corrective action. It is as though once a sin is committed, a string or tether is forever connected to that person and sticks with the individual, creating a sinful marionette that will continue to act and live with that attached sin.

In the age of Adam, sin was abolished simply by death, the sinful nature could not be overcome thus there was constant demand for sacrifice – that being the death of innocence – in order to atone for the sins of that time. It had been planned to send an ultimate sacrificial lamb as an act of mercy by God but prior to this happening, the abundant sin needed to be wiped from the Earth by flood and the time had to be right for such a lamb to be revealed to the world. Thus, Jesus Christ's crucifixion was the final sacrifice required to relinquish death's grip on sin. How?

God's fullest grace was placed into Mary upon her conception, she was brought into this world free of sin and by the fullness of God's mercy. She may have been human, but she lacked the usual sinful nature and mediocre faculties that we possess. Her blessed mission was to provide a human – one who would bear no sin and ultimately become the most perfect sacrifice to counter sin.

It was a two-step process – create Mary, free from sin, so that she could bear the Godman who would live a life without sin until His death, thus fulfilling the perfect sacrificial lamb. This act of mercy was provided by God and ended the sinful age of Adam where sin had been paid for by death.

The embodiment of God's mercy descended to Hell to recover the souls of the dead from the age of Adam and then rose again to Heaven. Christ defeated Death, an act of mercy that now allows the spirit of humans to bypass eternal death and instead find eternal life with Jesus showing the way. Therefore, the age of Adam was changed into the age of Christ. The sacrifice of blood and innocence was completed and today we live in an age of forgiveness and redemption.

Correcting Sin

Baptism removes our original sinful tether with which each person is born. After Baptism, as often as one sins, the tether of sin binds again but can be cut from the soul through divine grace found in confession and repentance. No longer do we have to live with the sins of our past until our dying day as long as we recognize that Christ's sacrifice was the ultimate payment for our sin, and as long as we acknowledge that we still do sin, and we pray contrition, confess our sins to God or the priesthood, and perform penance. The ties to sin always can be retied, but with full faith, full humility, and acceptance of our sinful nature, redemption is at hand. Do not squander the gift of eternal life for a blind and prideful life of sin.

Just as baptism is the initial step into a spiritual life, acknowledgment of one's own sinful nature is required before fully combatting the typical vices and temptations of sin. You cannot rightfully correct what is wrong in your life without first realizing that which is wrong.

Firstly, acknowledge the fall of humanity from God's original grace as the reason for a sinful human nature. Our purpose in the beginning was to be more than we are now, but upon committing the original sin, humanity has fallen from grace, just as the angels who opposed God's will fell from grace. The difference here is angels – possessing an intellect of eternity – make choices with irrevocable consequence. Humans – lacking such intelligence – are able to correct their actions.

Which leads to us correcting the sinful human condition – after acknowledgment of sin is performed, you must then recognize the consequence of sin. Sin separates us from God, just as is represented in the Fall. Denying sin is the same as denying God; you cannot be removed from the deception of denial without acknowledgment of the reality of sin, God, and judgment.

Bridging these points in time is life itself. We live from a birth of sin to a death with or without sin. That is exactly what having a life means and what we are currently achieving, but until the spiritual life born from baptism is established, a blind and deceived life would be the only life lived and would be met with a comparable judgment upon death.

It is terrifying to realize that despite having lived a life devoted to charity and kindness you may still be faced with just punishment for having denied God or Truth. We often believe that simply doing right, regardless of religious tendency, may be enough to save a soul upon death but carrying this personal judgment and predisposed perception is prideful and removes God's will from our lives. This is the deception plaguing most of the world today. Do not believe you can save yourself by being good – you need the intercession of divine mercy and grace. This is closer to truth than believing otherwise.

A Closing

Which leads us to a perceivably final point – how does one acquire divine mercy and grace such that sin can become lessened in life? To reduce the tendency to sin, one must persistently pray for such a freedom. One cannot remove himself or herself from sin alone. Upon baptism, let the spiritual regeneration commence through prayer and religious instruction.

Pray for God's will to allow you discretion, virtue, wisdom, and grace. Pray that the Blessed Mother Mary pray for you and align you with God's will. Pray for Jesus to redeem and save souls of the deceased as well as your own, that he may never leave your side. Ask for assistance from the saints and Angels who all act according to God's will. Profess your inherent sinful nature, acknowledge you are shameful and completely sinful, because you are – we all are.

And, above all, pray for forgiveness from the Holy and Almighty God the Father, that by His will you may find the proper fear in Him, grace from Him, and learn how to reciprocate love for Him, just as He has always intended to show humanity since the beginning.

DEMONOLOGY AND DISCOURAGING EVIL

The Confrontation

The will of God has been confronted by the will of humanity in a decisively one-sided battle; however, it is not purely the will of mankind spurring this confrontation. Our delusional sense of authority is the product of diabolical manipulation that is ironically permitted by the will of God. From those who remain oblivious to this truth, a blind conviction to serve the Satanic agenda emerges.

Humanity has failed to recognize in current times that the will of God supersedes all facets of our reasoning and perceptions. By possessing free will, we are able to internally disregard the will of God and cause the turmoil and defilement of our world and ourselves. The authority of God has allowed the authority of Satan to pervert the authority of humanity.

God used to be the center of our focus, similar to how we used to believe Earth was the center of the universe. As soon as we found comfort in the earth being suspended in a vast emptiness of space did we then begin to question the necessity of having God at the center of our lives. Just as Earth is hanging in the darkness so, too, does our dependence on God. We now have a direct division in the spirituality of ourselves. To address the issues and separation of the

Left-hand path and the Right-hand path, as well as the spiritual condition of our world, we will need to rekindle the factors that led us to today.

The Separation

Belief in anything is good for one's own soul, right? Perhaps to the individual perception, but only when the rejection and denial of pre-existing truths is harnessed does a semblance of growth appear. Not only does our world hang in utter darkness, so do the spiritual lives of those who believe anything prescribed by the intentions of this world. Our world is separated from God due to the inherent displeasure it causes God. We refer to this displeasure as sin, and it is what causes the further separation of individual souls from God.

Despite being removed from God, the divine faculties have not been omitted from our condition. We can still find divine grace, mercy, and intervention when requirements are met. This is performed through the acts of the Holy Spirit as well as the militant authority of God – that being the Angelic Order.

Angels are supernatural entities possessing intellect and will, just as we do, but of much higher degrees of acuity and perpetuity for they possess a perception of eternity. Thus, humans were not the first creation of God; angels existed prior to us – perhaps they too have their own legacy of discovering God's will and favor.

Today, we have our temporal realm in which humanity operates, angels operate, and where God's will and authority is projected on all. Where then does the ethical dilemma of evil come into play? If we believe everything of God is good, how does the ageless debate of good and evil even exist? Just as the world is separated from God due to sin, so can the wills of the created entities remove themselves from God's will. Two different variations of separation – one physically, the other mentally. The final separation would ultimately be spiritual, which is the truth of damnation, but first we discuss the physical and mental.

The Permittance of Evil

There is truth in God's will yielding good, but one must acknowledge everything that opposes or removes itself from this notion yields evil. Evil itself is the removal of God, the absence of God, or the rejection of God desired and granted by individual free will. Why does God permit evil to exist? Not only is God all good and benevolent, He is also so just and fair that He allows free will of his own creations, so much so that even they can choose to disapprove and reject Him, thus producing evil. God permits the mental will of his creations to act on their own terms because that is what is truly fair to existence.

When a person complains about suffering in the world, it is the complaint of an individual perception within an eternal timeline simply accounting for a perpetual accumulation of sin and evil that is currently affecting him or her at a specific point in time. Basically, the odds of not suffering are so against that person that it only makes sense that in a limited perception any hardship may be viewed as suffering or evil. This limited perception diminishes the intended purpose of allowing evil to occupy our realm, which is to serve as fundamental spiritual tests and build resolve within the spiritual nature of humanity.

If evil is the test of spirit, then shouldn't there also be a resource to fortify and strengthen the spirit? Not only is evil permitted to work within our realm but so is good. This is done by the Holy Spirit, angels, and those who abide by God's will, for those who turn towards God have already turned away from the rejection of God.

Evil has been an active force in the entirety of humanity – in order to see its origins, let's review religious origin.

In the Beginning

There once was a kingdom of God inhabited by God and his Angelic Orders. Upon revealing the creation of humans, God willed that, in time, he would take on flesh and guide them back to Him, for the Fall of mankind was already foreseen. Once the Angels heard that God would assume flesh for the salvation of humanity instead of taking on the spiritual body of an angel, a portion of the Angelic Order opposed this agenda. Humans are and always will be lesser than angels – why would God assume flesh? Not only this, but it was also revealed that the Son of God would ascend to Heaven and that all the Angels would glorify and praise that person as divinity.

Now this was the line, drawn and crossed. Who was then among the highest of the angels, Lucifer, raised a rebellion against God that yielded the committing of sin, the first moment of opposition to God's will. Thus, the third of the angels who rebelled against God were removed from heaven – for once such a sin is committed, it will not be permitted to remain in the presence of God. Lucifer and the angels who denied the will of God were eternally removed from God.

A characteristic of angels is their keen sense of perpetuity and perception of eternity. Because of this heightened sense, angels are able to see the specific outcomes of their own actions such that upon having decided to reject God's will, the angels were banished eternally without a chance of repentance or redemption. The notion of reconciliation is invalid for this band of angels who committed sin – they knew the exact consequence with which their decision would be met. They were to be spiritually removed from Heaven. To where were they sent?

Eternal punishment – Hell, Tartarus, Gehenna, Hades, the eternity of spiritual removal from God. This punishment was known by the angels who fell in that hour. To compare, when Adam and Eve committed the Original sin, humanity was too removed from God. A physical location was prepared for them, that being Earth, and a spiritual location was prepared for the fallen angels, that being Hell, both removed from God.

The Paradigm

So now we have our world, reserved for the repentance of man. God's mercy is so great that it provides humanity, possessing lower mental faculties than the angels, a chance for acknowledging sin, repenting, and ultimately gaining God's favor and grace again. Humans are lesser than angels in form and mind, but by God's mercy we have been elevated in regards to Grace. Then, there is a Hell, the reservation for damned souls who will eternally be removed from God if repentance and salvation not be found. And alas, there is Heaven – God's kingdom where His presence shines.

Although Earth is removed physically from God, there is still a mental and spiritual connection to Him, whereas Hell is physically, mentally, and spiritually removed from God. This overlap of connectivity brings us to the spiritual battle plaguing our world. God has permitted that because both Earth and Hell are physically removed from Him, the fallen angels can interact with the fallen state of humanity. Our free will is able to yield evil upon its rejection of God's will, and the fallen angels, whom have already eternally rejected God's will, are allowed to infiltrate our realm with their inherent evil.

Introduction to Demonology

This is how we have evil in our world, but it must abide by particular rules of engagement when acting in our world – a sort of spiritual politics. Evil is the multitude of fallen angels – whom we typically call demons – that primarily exploit the mental faculties of humanity to tempt, manipulate, and deceive us into committing sin. They also have access to our physical faculties, but this is only accomplished when the will of an individual is relinquished to the will of demons.

Thus, these are the limitations placed upon demons in our world – they can tempt and deceive us mentally, perhaps manipulate or exhibit physicality, but they can never interact with our spiritual nature in any way. This is because Earth is not removed from God spiritually – meaning God still exists within our spirit. Demons, being the eternal rejection of God, cannot intrude.

Demons are left to use their tools of deception to spur humans to sin and willfully reject and oppose God's will. Their goal is to have us believe God is unnecessary and ultimately bring the souls of humanity to damnation just as they have been judged – a pure example of malice and envy, for they despise that humans can acquire God's grace and a chance of atonement and redemption.

To remove popular notion immediately, one cannot sell his or her soul to the devil; it is not one's to give up, only God can make this decision. A person can will his or her mind and body be given to evil, but even this is usually caused by the unseen demonic forces of our world. This leads us to the tools available to evil – ordinary and extraordinary demonic activity.

Ordinary Activity

Detailing ordinary activity, the demons have access to our mental activity and faculties including imagination, dreams, and inclinations. Ordinary demonic activity is the daily battle against sinful actions and sinful thoughts. Demons can manipulate our cognitive approach to decisions, goals, and enacting our own will. It behooves one to be constantly vigilant and skeptical when sudden ideas or inclinations come to the forefront of the mind. Having strong mental fortitude to deter sinful thoughts, disposition to promote God's will, and desire to walk a righteous path can negate a majority of ordinary demonic activity.

Extraordinary Activity

Extraordinary demonic activity is the usual cause of direct willingness to interact with demons but can also be inadvertently experienced. Extraordinary activity is broken into four categories – infestation, vexation, obsession, and possession. The common theatrical representation of demonic forces may be exaggerated but accounts from exorcists yield that it is at times accurate. The difference between cinema and real life is that an actual battle over a human soul is occurring and the stakes are real.

Infestation

Demonic infestation occurs in association with a place or object. It could pertain to a home, building, room, items of value, items perceived to have power, or items of occult practice. The demons have more influence and freedom to act when within these particular places or when these objects are handled. In order for demons to believe they have such freedoms, they had to have gained acknowledgement, access, and permission to such physical affiliation. This consent can be given by God Himself or by humans who try to consort with evil or demons.

To reiterate, God can permit the extraordinary display of demonic force in order to further His good will, but in opposition to this, humans can also attempt to permit demonic activity in order to promote more sinister agendas. A person can act as a conduit for evil by first acknowledging the evil presence and then attempting to directly engage with it. If specific locations or items are excessively used to enact this demonic incitement, it is more likely a place can become demonically infested, causing future occurrences to happen either more regularly or more overtly.

Vexation

Having a demonic infestation merely means the demons can act more openly, but does not completely mean that the activities will be noticed. More noticeable demonic activity occurs in the other types of extraordinary activity, which are usually spurred by first being infested. Demonic vexation is the physical interaction of a demonic presence, such as moving or throwing of objects or even pushing and pulling individuals. The perceived freedom of the demon is so large in an infested place that it will openly display physical force.

Oppression

The more common occurrence, though, is demonic oppression – the direct mental attacks from a demonic entity. Vexation may physically assault, oppression may mentally assault. A mental intrusion will lead to rapid thoughts of obscenity, violence, the perversion of holiness, and possibly hallucinations, especially if drugs are being used.

Demonic oppression can be short and abrupt or can be prolonged in as much that the individual may suffer from a distorted memory, imagination, or inclination of thought. The true mood of the person can become affected to include rash violent outbursts, uncontrollable thoughts of murder, rape, suicide, sedition, sexual perversion, and impulsive behaviors, all of which may persist long after the initial demonic assault.

Demonic oppression is the real mental battleground that is comparatively associated with mental disease and mental disorder. Understand here that common psychologists who do not accept nor include the possibility of demonic oppression are already losing the battle. You cannot have a science based purely on human perception when the true evil lurking in the mind can remain hidden from the senses. It may be uncomfortable to admit, but I believe most of us have been victims of demonic influence. Predisposition to evil thoughts and sudden changes in mood must have the diagnosis of demonic oppression as a possibility.

Possession

Demonic possession is the rarest of extraordinary cases reported, but I will later suggest not for transparent reasons. To define possession, it occurs when the consistent individual will has openly acknowledged and permitted demonic forces to act freely so much that the personal will of the individual is relinquished to the will of the demonic force. While this can be done with intention, it is usually the negligent result of dealing with spiritual matters unknown to the person.

It is here that I will provide the premise of black magic and summoning demons as well as what it actually accomplishes. Demons are given permission to act within limitations set forth by God and God alone. The world is not mankind's kingdom nor paradise, it has been handed over to Satan for the purposes of testing true faith and spiritual resolve. The authority of Satan has been permitted to use any and all practices of deceit to fully challenge the will of humanity. This results in the perfect deception, for without this knowledge, a person grows up a child of the world and believes his or her own will and sovereignty is absolute.

The demons use this ignorance of truth to deceive us into believing that what we will is actually what occurs. Black magic and consorting with demons breaks the first commandment, beginning the separation of one's will from God's will. It also allows for easier access to our mental faculties such that one might be handing him or herself over to evil without fully realizing it. This is the trick – to make one believe that his or her own will can command demons or gain power through demonic force. Do not believe your will is superior to the will of any other will, for it is not, not even to the will of the demons trying to bring you to damnation.

Thus, when demonic possession occurs, it is either willed by God, or performed by the complete submission of the individual's will to that of the demon. Demons are fallen angels; they are not little minions or imps like popularly characterized. They still have the full intellect and attributes of the Angelic Order; it is just that the divine spirit is removed from them and their will is in pure opposition to God. They will always be superior to humans regarding intellect. Regardless of result from any form of black magic or consorting with demons, it is all simply their trap to lure you into believing your own will is supreme.

Therefore, demonic possession occurs by accident, such as when one gets submerged too quickly into spiritual realities, but also by intent, because the person believes that it is he or she commanding the demons. This leads me to believe not all demonic possessions are fully recorded. The victim of demonic deceit would appropriately seek assistance; the possession warranted by intent of a participant might not.

When an individual is possessed by demons, some or even all physical faculties of the body are surrendered to the will of the demon such as limbs, memories, or the tongue. The body is no longer under the full authority of the person and can lead to convulsions, contorting of the body, and even the speaking of unknown phrases or languages.

When this possession is fully and intentionally willed by the individual for purposes internalized by that person – usually the perverted notion of power or curiosity – the fullness of the body is taken over by the demon or demons. This is called a perfect possession. If this occurs, it is possible for the person to act normally while under complete control of demonic forces. I can only imagine what occurs behind closed doors. These cases will most likely go unnoticed and probably do not represent the fullness of recorded demonic possessions. Those who realize their fault will seek assistance; those who believe they are in control would not.

Conclusion to Demonology

In all, this would serve as a fair conclusion of the most common and apparent situations of demonic activity and the tools utilized by evil in spiritual conflict. Remember, the reason God permits evil on Earth is because we are already physically separated from God, and it serves as a spiritual test to form resolve and fortitude, thus ultimately serving a greater good. The only intent of fallen angels or demons is to bring as many human souls to damnation as possible through the perversion of our minds and will.

If you find yourself immediately in need of resolution to a perceived demonic situation in your life, I will note here briefly to always remember God's will is supreme, that in God's will you must maintain faith and hope, and always pray God's will may bring you to righteousness and sanctification. Also, you should pray for the intercession of the Blessed Mother Mary to align you with God's will and pray that Jesus remain with you in body, mind, and spirit. We will discuss further tactics to discouraging evil and combatting sin shortly.

Evil of the Past

Although we attribute demons to having a particular power within our realm today, what was their mode of operation in the past? Today the primary focus is on the perversion of mind and will but what of ages past? Take into perspective the formation of the world in regards to the lineages of humanity proceeding Adam. If we start with creation, Adam and Eve were tempted to commit the Original sin of disobeying God. How was Satan able to tempt or impart an evil will upon Eve? If at that time they existed in the presence of God, how could evil have affected them?

The simple answer is the Fall of humanity was already known to God such that His plan of providing a way for us to find redemption was already in motion. When the plan of assuming flesh and leading humanity back to God was revealed, the Fall of the Angels occurred – effectively causing the fallen angels to curse the grace bestowed upon humans and to swear bringing about the damnation of them. Thus, Satan was the first test of human obedience towards God.

When the inevitable Original sin was committed, mankind was separated from God; sin is not permitted to exist within the sanctity of God's presence. However, the will and spirit of God was still among them – even Adam and Eve regretted having committed sin. Thus, following the Fall, we have a whole lineage of humans proceeding Adam being born into the sinful state that was the consequence of sin but still able to appease this sinful nature through sacrifice. But evil was also present.

The fallen state of humanity was growing in sin while also under the influence of evil – the beginning stages of a perpetual spiritual war were being established. Imagine a battleground full of ill-equipped humans with improper mental faculties, inherent inclination to sin, and an unfortified spirit facing the pure malice of supernatural fallen angels sworn to devious motives of corrupting man. How more one-sided could it have been? In this era, an immensity of sin prevailed; it appeared that evil was winning the battle over mankind's salvation.

The fallen angels went as far as conceiving children with the human women in order to pollute the population even further. This incestuous sin prevailed until the accumulation of sin was so abundant that an ultimate judgment of God was passed to eradicate the sin of the world – the Flood. The renewal of the land and people would not be in vain, for the next age of humanity would eventually receive Jesus as a savior.

Another realization is that this new age of mankind would persist well beyond the Flood, even up until this day – no more would God use such destructive force to wipe away the sins of the world. This also meant the operations of the fallen angels needed to change, for they were aware of the coming Christ. How could they progress their plans of global damnation?

The distortion of human minds was key to having Christ's coming less effective – the demons needed to place faith and belief in the world that would rival Christ. Thus, polytheistic religions - Sumerian, Egyptian, Norse, Celtic, Greek, Roman, Persian, Hindu pantheons, and many more – spread like wildfire throughout a world divided by large distance and a multitude of language. These belief systems are all perversions of the one true God's individual power and are most likely reflections of demonic entities revealed to the minds and imaginations of the people. The demons had a field day planting the seeds of distorted truths that would sprout into the polytheistic religions still studied and believed today. A perpetual paganism was formed and has been a constant combatant against the salvation of souls.

Evil of Today

Throughout time, the minds of humans have been a battleground between Truth and distorted truths. Today we are primarily left with the *big three* monotheistic religions of the world – Christianity, Islam, and Judaism. Amidst the chaos and turmoil of polluted doctrines, beliefs, stories, and religions, we as humanity, by God's grace and mercy, have preserved the closest to Truth within these three fields of piety – but the battle is not near resolution. Today's demonic agenda is to cripple these religious foundations from within – Christian schisms caused by technicalities of salvation, Muslims arguing over worldly sovereignty and lineage, and Jews denying Christ as savior despite having been the chosen people of God to prophesy such a coming.

It is typical to recognize these three religions as primary in our world due to geography and concentration, but I will address the arising Buddhism and Eastern Asian schools of thought briefly. In essence, the Asian community has developed a sense of an internal enlightenment that attributes harmony and peace of the world to the inner confines of the mind. At face value, this is quite a beautiful representation of the effects we as humanity can have on the world around us. Its constant striving for inner peace yields liberation from evil thought and deed. It is a self-found grace that is desired to be imparted on the world. The issue with this practice is that it not only removes evil, it also removes the Holy Spirit and God from working within the earthen vessel. They are basically the closest, at apex, to a self-made god that a human could be. This unfortunately removes God's will from their own, ultimately becoming more sinful then spiritually beneficial. The mind is there, but the spirit is not.

Our focus here though is on the true forces at work, that being the mystical body of Christ represented through the Catholic Church and the malcontent intentions of Satan enacted by demonic forces. These two conflicting forces have kindled the world in which we live today. We are in a confused state consequent of ages of spiritual warfare where now we have so much to potentially believe that we get lost. How can anyone decipher which truths have been upheld? With what does one spiritually align? The harsh reality is that humanity has failed itself through generations of deception being taught as truth.

A god of war and destruction? Sure, I can believe in that. Multiple gods? Makes sense. Women? The single most important gateway of souls into this world? Might as well devalue and belittle them. A political body representing the removal of one's will from God's? Yes, please, because God is dead after all, but I'm alive now. I think therefore I am, and that is godliness to me! In fact, let's separate church from state, we don't need that ancient archaic nonsense to govern our society. What good ever came from loving your neighbors and not committing adultery and polluting generations of our children? We are men, not slaves, no longer will we abide by religious doctrine for now we have science and technology! There is no more room for God even if He does live. Everything man needs, man provides. Sin? I do as I please. Just like Franky, I did it my way and will continue to do it my way. My will is all that matters anymore!

And thus, Original sin and the inclination to sin has beheld generations of men and women devoid of acknowledging God's existence, God's will, and God's mercy. They were, and we are, subjecting future generations to damnation without even realizing the truth of our own actions. Our society has become so demonized that we, ourselves, promote our own damnation. It is as if a sinful snowball was formed in the early stages of humanity and just grew and grew until now even the demons just sit back and watch us fall away from God.

The sheep of God have wandered away from their true shepherd and are marching right into the wolves' den. This is the consequence of demonic activity in our world. It has yielded countless souls to fight a terrible spiritual battle without the acknowledgment of divine resources available. Fighting depression, addiction, lust, avarice, compulsive acts, perversion, and faith – all alone. What greater tragedy could exist than the losing of one's own spiritual battle?

How was humanity supposed to avoid this concupiscent and sinful nature? It was meant to be the duty of elders and the educated or wise to uphold and maintain such truths regarding God and mankind, but it seems time has slowly decayed the outreach that was once common. Perhaps there were just too many people and not enough elders. Perhaps the term educated took on a more worldly view in today's society, one where the salvation of taxes and efficacy of production is more intelligent than the salvation of souls and efficacy of prayer.

Whatever allowed for the acceptance of such a direct rupture in humanity's identity, the generations of the past failed to instill proper values and faith in the new generations – at least on a large scale. It is the duty of parents and grandparents to ensure proper paths of life are passed on, not a complacent and blind admission of the times. Time and the ages of humanity will change; Truth will not.

But who can really be blamed in a realm confronted with such chaotic and supernatural forces at work? The demons held a grasp on just enough of humanity to ensure death begot death and the sanctity of lies was the inheritance of newer generations. But by God's mercy and will, just enough of truth has been preserved to keep redemption at hand. It just takes a little hardening of the soul, weakening of pride, and realigning of the will in order to bring us back to the light. No matter how deep or dark a path one has walked, the fork in the road is always present. Have faith in this.

For that is the true glory of God, His sheep are always welcome back to the heavenly flock; it just takes acknowledgment of this truth. Profess the sinful nature in which you live, acknowledge God, His judgment, and redemption in Jesus, and find strengthening of the spirit through prayer and the sacraments.

These are the lessons that should have been passed down through the generations, not perceptions of seizing the world by one's own will. The kingdom of God is not of this world. Why would you instill in your children to seize the kingdom of this world? Worldly desire is without doubt the Satanic agenda; steer away from these notions and pray that you may be filled with the spirit of fear of the Lord.

Discouraging Evil

We have come to a point where instruction on how to combat demonic forces is proper. We have seen from where evil comes, its purpose and intention in past and present, and what effects it has had on humanity. I will briefly discuss how to combat extraordinary demonic activity, for it is primarily the Catholic Church, but also ordinary demonic activity such as urges, impulses, and thoughts, then finally how to live a life that will limit both of these unnecessary altercations from occurring. Cleansing of the mind and soul is near, even for you who believe to be damned already.

Catholic Authority

If you truly believe to be the victim of extraordinary demonic activity – infestation, vexation, oppression, or possession – you should contact the Catholic Church in order to get in touch with the Archdiocese of your area. Only ordained Catholic priests who have been trained to deal in demonic activity and exorcism have the authority to begin proper inquiry and investigation.

This authority has been represented and passed down through tradition within the Church by the laying on of hands, starting back from Jesus Christ Himself. Jesus carried strict rule over demonic force and once he passed the authority of His Church to the Apostles, that strict rule was passed too. The Catholic Church has maintained this tradition for every ordained priest through the sacrament of Holy Orders.

Do not try to get rid of any demonic forces with direct confrontation on your own because it can exacerbate the phenomenon. Your interaction can give it the validation necessary to become worse. In conjunction with contacting the Catholic Church, you may also begin renewing your mind and life with the following steps meant to combat ordinary demonic activity.

Confronting Sin

The internal battle of the demonic is personal, for your mind acts as a sanctuary for yourself as long as you understand its role in communion with God. In order to combat ordinary activity inflicting your mind or mood, you must bring yourself closer to a state of grace with God, meaning that your sins have been forgiven and that you can begin anew with a hardened spirit granted by God's mercy. In most cases, the removal of sin and the inclusion of pious acts will significantly reduce ordinary demonic activity.

Thus, the first step – stop sinning! To the best of your willing human nature, stop committing conscious sin. The habits of sin must be broken. To many, committing sin may go unnoticed or even overlooked because of its perceived insignificance. All sin is opposition to God's will and law; some sins are harsher than others. Do not believe that you have a right to sin. Although we sin daily, it is prideful to believe we simply have a right to do such.

Venial Sin

Venial sins are lower violations and consist of seemingly subconscious acts such as doing too much of a recreational activity like watching tv or playing games, eating more than was necessary, speeding down a highway, thinking a nasty thought, or missing prior obligations. These are sins that can minorly affect yourself or others. Regardless of the seeming insignificance, it is a distortion of regular order.

Grave Sin

Grave sin is of a harsher degree and consists of abrasive and rash violations of God's will and law. In regard to daily life, these include impulsive violence, willed malevolent thoughts, sexual perversion such as masturbation or lustful thoughts, stealing, skipping church mass without proper reason, reaching an excessive drunkenness, or even acting purely on emotion, which usually leads to regret. These are the sins that result from a lack of discipline and control, a lost temper, a disregard for consequence, or a passionate impulse.

Mortal and Unforgiveable Sin

Mortal sin is any grave sin committed with direct will and knowledge of its sinful causality. Intent as well as practice elevate the severity of the sin committed. Mortal sin of the highest severity is known as unforgiveable sin and is the direct opposition to the Holy Spirit. This is typically done through impenitence, but also by willfully refusing or resisting revealed truths, or even believing that one's own sin is greater than the mercy of God.

Although called "unforgiveable sin," God's mercy and intervention may cause a miracle in one's own spiritual realization, but the truth of these sins is that without deliberate penitence the individual is literally bringing him or herself to damnation. Always remember God's mercy is greater than your own sinful nature and previous misdeeds so that you may pray for the forgiveness of your sins.

Seven Deadly Sins

The seven deadly sins capture the majority of sinful activities we can commit. Therefore, I will list them all, give examples, and provide the virtue that counters them. If you find yourself inflicted with a particular order of sin, pray for the virtue that can combat it; do not fight your sinful nature alone – you can never win. Ask, pray, and meditate on the virtuous practice that you need.

Pride

Pride is the belief that your will supersedes God's will. What you want and demand of the world shall be given to you without the need of God. This is also the derivative of believing that you do not need to repent nor need God's mercy for salvation. Any notions that put yourself at the center of your own life should be abandoned. The virtue of humility counters pride.

Envy

Envy is the hateful spite of another based on what they possess – physically, mentally, or spiritually. Demons possess pure envy of humanity for having access to God's grace and redemption. The direct feelings of contempt towards another cultivates opposition to loving thy neighbor and should be replaced with an understanding of individual circumstance. The virtue of kindness counters envy.

Avarice

Avarice is the unreasonable or hastened desire of riches or worldly fame. The more one craves the fruits of the world, the less receptive to the fruits of the spirit one becomes. Always wanting more than what you actually need can cause an endless desire to become master of the world instead of the desire to seek God and wisdom. Do not become a child of the world; remain a child of God. The virtue of charity counters avarice.

Lust

Lust is the desire for sensual pleasure and is usually formulated in the mind before any action is made. The overt fascination of sex or one's body becomes idolatry and clouds one's relationship with God. Lust will lead to sexual perversion, masturbation, and on impulse rape or assault. One must keep discretion over the mind in order to subdue urges and always remember to keep God the focus of life. The virtue of chastity counters lust.

Gluttony

Gluttony is the excessive consumption of things or time. It disregards moderation and focuses on the satisfaction one receives from food, recreational activity, or drugs and alcohol. One substitutes the demand for God's love and grace with the demand for instant-gratification and worldly sensation. The virtue of temperance counters gluttony.

Sloth

Sloth is the lacking of motivation or will to do for yourself, for others, or more importantly, for God. Depression and fatigue can cause adverse effects in one's behavior, which may lead to lethargy, but remember that even prayer or going to church can be just enough action needed to satisfy your spirit. If a task seems overwhelming, keep faith in God and know you will not be alone in your endeavors. The virtue of diligence counters sloth.

Malice

Malice is the deliberate inclination towards violence, aggression, and hatred. This usually spurs from misunderstanding or the rejection of truth. Do not be a victim of passion or emotion. Maintain the discipline and countenance of one who can control him or herself. When facing adversity, meet it with understanding and humility, not impulsive rage. The virtue of patience counters malice.

Summary of Sin

Sin comes in many forms and all sin is not the same. The intent to sin is more severe than the accidental sin. Habitual sin is more damning than the sporadic sin. The sin of one's own fault is more excusable than the sin of one's own rejection of truth. Understanding sin and what practices and virtues subdue it is key to becoming not just a better person among your peers but also becoming a true child of God. Venial sins are forgiven communally at church and mass. Grave and mortal sins must be confessed to a confessor. If confession is unavailable, fervent prayers of contrition can take place of confession until one can partake in the sacrament of confession. Pray constantly for forgiveness. Pray constantly for wisdom. And pray constantly for mercy and grace.

Embracing Effective Prayer

Which leads us to the next action in order to combat ordinary demonic activity – prayer. When told to pray, many may not understand exactly what to pray for or even how to pray. Efficiency of prayer varies based on your state of grace and also how repentant or mortified your soul is.

Becoming closer to a state of grace is achieved by having sin removed from your current state, meaning you have been baptized to remove Original sin, you have performed the sacrament of confession to remove mortal sin, and you have been to mass to remove venial sin. Basically, Catholics compete to see how long they can maintain a state of grace before sinning again – I typically make it 'til noon. Fervent penitence is met with mortification of the soul – even fasting for one day can amplify your prayers. You must put yourself into a humbled, pious, and willing submission to God's mercy – this is how to find more efficiency in prayer.

Pacing and routing of prayer is also important. Saying the words with intent, belief, and a steady pace helps keep you within a train of thought – one does not want to hurry to a stumbling of words. Take time and have faith that even God will help you pray for what you need appropriately. Also knowing what heavenly resources are available to you – purely ready to assists you spiritually – will help your prayer have more substance. Praying through the saints, the Angelic Order, the Blessed Virgin Mary, the Son of God Jesus Christ, and ultimately placing you and your petition or prayer at the mercy of the Father, God Almighty will more effectively feel complete when you finish a prayer.

Vocal prayer is typically that which is done in mass and gatherings also called the liturgy. It places the petitions of God's people at the mercy of God's will. This is an effective way to cover multiple concerns at once and to let the voices of the faithful be heard clearly. This is why church is so important – imagine all the world giving their prayers throughout a day.

A Template of Prayer

Personal prayer is individual and will be different from person to person – it's the internal voice we use to reach out and find grace. While different for everyone, templates have been prepared such as Jesus providing the "Our Father" prayer and many more passed down by Catholic mystics and saints. I will provide a template of routing, which I tend to use frequently.

Always open with the sign of the cross, "In the name of the Father, and of the Son, and of the Holy Spirit. Amen." This opens the immediate acknowledgement of the Holy Trinity and exposes you to the working of the Holy Spirit.

"Insert here" an intercessory prayer for the Blessed Mother of God, the Queen of Heaven, Mary. Holy Mary acts as an intermediary and is very important to acknowledge having on your side. Pray that she prays for you and assist you by God's will.

Then "insert here" recognition of the Lamb of God and Redeemer of Souls Jesus Christ, whom takes away the sins of the world and brings redemption and salvation. Welcome and pray that Jesus be with you in body, mind, and in spirit now and always.

And ultimately pray to our Father – the Almighty and Holy One True God whose love, mercy, and presence is beyond comprehension. Profess your humility and unworthiness as a humble servant of God, and confess your sinful nature to God's Mercy. Pray for forgiveness, grace, and that God's will move you along the path of righteousness and wisdom.

Within this template, you will find the time and placement for individual circumstance. Always preface your desire or will with "May God will that…" or "By God's will…" in order to always put God before yourself. He will ensure what is right and proper for you will be done. It is important to pray for others as well, for not all people have the humility or even time to pray with fervor and meaning. Prayer is not just your personal petition; it can also be your asking of grace and mercy for others. Without the monasteries and convents around the world consistently praying for each one of us, I don't know in what state we would be.

Prayer Works

Demons despise that which is holy – Jesus, Mary, divine grace, divine mercy, and even just sinners praying for forgiveness. The fallen angels cannot be redeemed so it brings them agony when they hear those who they want damned receiving and giving prayers of forgiveness and repentance. Purge and purify your mind and spirit with incessant prayers of forgiveness, Mary's intercession, and Jesus' salvation all lifted up to the Father God Almighty. Then fortify your spirit by praying for wisdom, grace, mercy, and virtue so future battles of sin become easier.

Regardless of what you pray for, always place your faith and hope in God, Jesus, and Mary. If you believe demonic forces are interrupting your spiritual growth, you can research and find template Catholic deliverance and intercessory prayers that can help relieve the evil influences. Remember, the more virtuous you hope to be, the less afflicted you will become.

Importance of Mass

The third action of countering ordinary demonic activity is simply attending church. One cannot be free of sin nor follow a path of religious instruction without the easiest method – mass. Going to church achieves forgiveness of your minor sin and also allows you to become closer to the presence of holiness. It is revitalizing to the spirit and also necessary, since missing church is actually a sin. The church can also offer resources for instruction such as bible studies or the provision of a confessor or spiritual director. Demons want to bring you further from God so that you are more vulnerable. Counter this by running right into His love and grace by attending public mass.

The Ten Commandments

To conclude the actions meant to combat demonic activity, we will finish with what it means to live a righteous and spiritually rewarding life. Demonic influence is lessened when the entirety of a life is dissolved in the righteous laws of God and focused on the advancement of the spiritual self. Specific demonic influence might be more apparent at times, but the negation of sin is always the first step to removing the effects of evil. The next step is living right by the Ten Commandments and adopting a life pleasing to God. Every day can be a joyous representation of our love for God when living within His laws. This tends to ward off evil forces because the more one seeks God's favor, the more their spirituality is lifted and grace is granted, thus removing the direct ties to demonic forces.

You shall have no other gods before me (Exodus 20:3 NRSV)

This is among the most important commandment because violation of it is the direct mental willingness to deny God in place of someone or something else. Whether worshiping a person, a valuable item, even money, or another spiritual entity, one must remember that God is greater than all – thus deserves fullness of conviction and glory. The sins that compete with this commandment are pride, avarice, and lust.

You shall not make for yourself an idol (Exodus 20:3 NRSV)

This commandment coincides with the first but expands to the physical creation of idols of worship. These could include pagan statues or even lucky charms. Any item created contrary to the glory of God is something designed to divert one's attention from God. The sins that compete with this commandment are pride and avarice.

You shall not make wrongful use of the name of the Lord (Exodus 20:7 NRSV)

This commandment holds two concepts. One must not inappropriately use the Lord's name such as in swearing, but also one must not test God meaning to demand action. This directs us to properly use God's name through prayer and to also have faith in everything that He does. The sins that compete with this commandment are envy, avarice, and malice.

Remember the Sabbath day, and keep it holy (Exodus 20:8 NRSV)

Go to church. Mass is mandatory and not going because of insignificant reasons results in a mortal sin. Mass is the public and communal gathering of praise to God and also serves as spiritual instruction and a chance to have venial sin forgiven. The sins that compete with this commandment are pride and sloth.

Honor your father and your mother (Exodus 20:12 NRSV)

God's grace worked through your parents to allow for your coming into this world; do not squander the recognition of their efforts – show gratitude. The fulfillment of your birth is to be remembered and respected as having been the working of God as well as your mother and father. This also serves as a good practice of the virtue of obedience. The sins that compete with this commandment are pride and malice.

You shall not murder (Exodus 20:13 NRSV)

Taking of life is reserved for God's will and should not be committed under misguided intention. There is no sanctity in war or crime. Remember obeying a lawful order is an act of obedience but always pray for forgiveness. When one threatens your well-being, it is without doubt the influence of the demonic, for no person of God would stoop to such action. Protect yourself, for you are a temple of

God under attack. The sins that compete with this commandment are envy and malice.

You shall not commit adultery (Exodus 20:14 NRSV)

The sacrament of marriage is sacred and should not be interrupted even if the marriage is not done in accordance to Christian faith. The melding of two persons is a unity comparable to communion with God, for love begets love. There is no justification of ruining a marriage without receiving a proper annulment. The sins that compete with this commandment are envy, lust, and gluttony.

You shall not steal (Exodus 20:15 NRSV)

God provides and takes away. You should not overrule God's will in dispersing to each what is just. While stealing usually pertains to items, also think of what else can be stolen from another – time, emotion, effort, or even faith. The sins that compete with this commandment are envy and gluttony.

You shall not bear false witness against your neighbor (Exodus 20:16 NRSV)

Rumors and gossip are a Satanic practice such that they often spread lies or deceit usually to incite the passions of others. Abiding by this commandment prevents the ruination of relationships. The sins that compete with this commandment are envy and malice.

You shall not covet (Exodus 20:17 NRSV)

This means that you should not keep desires for the possessions or relationships that do not belong to you. This commandment is the direct removal of envy in an individual and places true faith in God's actions and will. Do not let yourself be overcome by emotions because of circumstances outside of your own control. The sins that compete with this commandment are envy, lust, and avarice.

These brief descriptions of the commandments ought to bring one closer to fulfilling a life of righteousness as well as limiting demonic influence. They are meant to be remembered and instilled in daily practice constantly and for the duration of a life. Should you recognize your breaking of a certain commandment, pray contrition and for forgiveness, go to confession, and prevent further sins of such nature by praying for the appropriate virtue and wisdom.

A Closing

Life is a puzzle, and the pieces can get lost sometimes or perhaps never even discovered. Fortunately, God's mercy and desire to have you seek Him and His righteousness always allow the puzzle pieces to be found and put in their proper place. Should sin corrupt the finished product, always turn towards the Blessed Mother Mary, Jesus Christ, and the Holy Father for guidance and forgiveness.

When we remove the unnecessary temptations and sins from our life, we can use more proper discretion and prudence when confronting future sin. Be mindful that regardless of virtue or inclination to seek God, one may still be tested by God in order to yield spiritual growth and a greater good. At times, the spiritual tests may feel like evil itself is your only associate, and it may be, but always by God's will. In these moments, it may feel as though God has abandoned you – do not fall into the tempting traps of believing such. Accept any joy or any hardship with full conviction and devotion towards God, and God alone, for He is the only way out of any despair and darkness.

Should God cast you into the pits of Hell, maintain a steadfast love and acceptance of His will – it is always righteous and just.

AN INTERPRETATION OF LOVE

God is love (1 John 4:8 NRSV)

How has such a simple expression, such a simple formula, such a simple truth become so misunderstood and forgotten? Through ages of humanity, we have substituted and reformed the actual meaning of this phrase. We have dissected the reality of this statement and forced it to match the notions and popularities of our time. Slowly we have turned God is love into God is love – as long as you even want to believe in God, and also as long as the love being represented is one in which all can agree because love is now subjective, it's not universal, it changes based on your identity and tendency.

But, no. We do not choose the basis of this statement. We have no right. It was already defined before our twisted perceptions ripped apart what the meaning of love actually is. It was already exemplified prior to our thoughts conceiving the notion that maybe God doesn't even exist. Defined and exemplified by that God whom we question – the Father.

God is love has become a confused concept because we forget who God is, we forget what love even is, and we disregard that the statement is written in the present tense – it does not change. I am who I am. (Exodus 3:14 NSRV) God is love. It is indicative of an eternal relationship, possibly the first relationship relative to our existence. God, the Father, is love.

What love is being represented? The love of worldly things? The love of sensual pleasure? The love of ourselves over others? If it is the purest form of love, then it could never be any of these lowly perceptions of love. It's the type of love that instills joy unconditionally. It's the type of love that brings gratitude constantly. It's the type of love that bonds eternally. It is the true love of a Creator and of His creation, unyielding and limitless, a love worthy of complete sacrifice and of complete commitment.

To us humans, we have been given the fullness of this love without really understanding or realizing it. Most of us have a hard time even reciprocating it. Alas, that is exactly what the pureness of this love truly is – it is always present, it is always crying out, and it is always ready to be received. It does not require a certain status; it does not require a certain time; there is no prerequisite for it; it has been fully radiant since your birth and please believe, even far before that.

It is like the selfless love that forms the first time you place eyes on your newborn child. The love that cries out, *"I made this?! But it is so perfect! I want to cherish it and preserve it! I want it to grow up and realize exactly how much I love it!"* It is formed instantaneously and lasts forever. This is real love, not the false love that is only shared on days that we get along, nor the love that comes only after I do something for you, nor the love that disappears as soon as something hurtful is said.

No other love is greater than God's love, and this rests in the truth that He is the exact love that any of us experiences – even if for a moment. The love we find in our child, the love we remember when our spouse originally said *"yes,"* the love we have over our family and friends. It is not all just a perceived euphoria – it is a piece of that boundless love which is God being experienced. Once one truly wishes to seek God and find in Him the endless love spurred by Creation, then a truer sense of a fulfilling and overwhelming love can be found.

We don't generate love between one another – we simply find God's love. Love already exists in everything He has made – the love that is exhibited by the master craftsman once a great work is completed. The painter, the architect, the potter, the blacksmith, the Father. This love for each and every created piece is personal, for each piece has required a little bit more or a little bit less of the artist. Specific blemishes and faults, unnoticed method and technique, the hidden gems and skill – these are all known by the Creator. Eventually they are discovered by the created and then able to be appreciated by all, but it is the personal trials of making such a creation unique that is fully felt by the artist. That fullness of love is inherent in every single one of us. There is a connection between each of us and God, and it is love.

Do you squander the love given to you? Do you seek love in the places you never find it? Believe that there is no greater joy than recognizing just how deep God's love really is. In this world, we focus heavily on physical love. Lasting relationships learn to love the minds of one another, but what relationship carries the concern for the spirit of each other? Regardless of our senses and peace of mind, the spirit must find love as well as be loved. Nothing of this world achieves spiritual love other than God's love, and no reciprocal love is more enjoyed by Him than that of a soul aware of and receptive to His love.

It is the very nature of love itself – the eternal communion of two spirits without concern or worry of anything whatsoever. Selfless, unconditional, eternal love is only found in the spirit. The sensual and mental head games we play in our lives are just meant to fill the void until we become wise enough to realize it.

Relationships not focused on God are destined to fail. So many will argue that they have been married for decades and are still madly in love even though God is not their focus. They are not failing love, are they? Alas, failure is seen in multiple ways. Has your marriage yielded the salvation of both of your souls, or have you not focused on that yet? Have your children been raised on a path that will help them find God, or have you thrown them to the wolves yelling that they fend for themselves?

Perhaps the most merciful of failed marriages are the ones that end so abruptly. At least they have a chance to figure out what true love is – the right way – and before they become devoted to a life and marriage that will always keep God out of focus. One does not have a true love for another if the simple concern of that person's soul never even arises. It is impossible to claim a full love for another with only the considerations of the body and mind.

The sanctity of marriage is a foundation for promoting spiritual love, not carnal lust. It is a platform on which the pillars of the family can stand, not where the cracks and ruptures of illegitimacy and infidelity appear. If you look upon your spouse and do not think of two things – God and her soul – you have no love. You are not a man if you cannot put God before your marriage nor if you cannot put your spouse before yourself. If you have children without the intention of teaching them about virtue and love, you are failing them and yourself. If you look at your child and don't even consider the salvation of his or her soul, then you are not a parent – you are a jailer. You are holding that poor child hostage until he or she becomes wise enough solely by God's mercy or until he or she learns truth from someone who actually cares. The parents who collectively disregard the physical, mental, and spiritual well-being of their children are an abomination and complete disgrace to the truth that they have so quickly abandoned – that God is love.

What is it when one experiences love? It's when you feel comforted. It's when you feel consoled. It's when you feel protected. It's when you feel liberated. It's when you never feel alone. It's when you find the joy in little things. It's when you can freely empathize with a companion. It's when you are promised something by another and believe it will be. It's when one smiles and you feel it. It's when one dies and they are still forever with you.

Love is the spark of hope and joy that meets every instance of despair and fear and completely wipes that negativity away – those moments in time when the greatest comfort and consolation bring us out of the darkness and places us right where we should be. This is what love is for us – within the limited faculties of our reception of it. It is those instances that bring you to your knees with eyes full of tears. This is love.

It is painful and joyous. It is pure submission yet a firm unbending. It is powerful as well as merciful. It is the summit of dualities because it is the connection that demands one to give all and another to take all. Should that love be reciprocated, then the all received is returned and an endless, eternal love can be had.

Is it a shame that we as humans perceive love while only experiencing it on a smaller scale than its actuality? How miserable must we be when we believe to have found love and can only enjoy it for a moment before another facet or desire of life take it away! Or rather, what a blessing it is to feel any sense of such an eternal connection at all. It may be the only sense of eternity available to us at all! That is how endless love truly is, that it, being removed from time and being itself eternal, can still be felt within our mortal lives.

How great and fulfilled is he who has experienced a portion of it! For in that brief moment of love, when the world paused and you looked around at your surroundings, and then back again at your companion. You smiled, perhaps the biggest smile of your life, and maybe just internally, not actually with the mouth, but you felt it. You felt love. You felt God. And it caressed your soul. And it lingered, but eventually the world interfered as it always does. The waitress came to take your order, or maybe it was already time to pay, or maybe in the distance you could hear the ambulance sirens, and suddenly your senses stole your lasting emotion. Your lasting spiritual love. And now – it's just a memory. Even as you're sitting right here with her, it's already a memory.

For such is love. It comes and goes, at least for us. Even God just passes through from time to time, reminding each of us that He loves us. When this happens how do we react? Most will probably deny God the proper gratitude, some will give thanks, and the rest will fall victim to a love so good but so short that they will fail to acknowledge the utility in it. We get to see glimpses of the eternal love that waits for each of us to retrieve it – this piece of the whole is sometimes too painful to bear. The impatient want it all now; the humble don't even believe they deserve it at all. What does it take to find love and to keep it?

You have to remember from where love comes. We feel the incitement of the emotions by grace but also by our own perspectives and outlook. When we use proper discretion and discernment, joy and love can become even more joyous and even more beautiful. Don't let the world strip you of your sentiment and spiritual growth. Instead, let your spiritual growth rob you of your senses – this is how to remove the worldly perception and expectation of things. The world and its entirety – people, animals, nature, the phenomena associated with natural order – were all handcrafted by God. Surely you can find beauty, appreciation, and love somewhere in that.

And when you do, don't be disheartened when that moment of love comes to pass. Cherish the memory and always remember that God's love is unending. The mere glimpse you had of this truth will resonate more soundly within you that maybe you can even maintain a peaceful joy until you open your eyes to another display of love – and of God.

JUDGMENT IS FINAL

Our society has become accustomed to a justice that is fluid and dynamic. As common notion changes, as interpretation of the law changes, as regular technology changes, our system of justice evolves and becomes more popularly accepted. Even the sentencing of an individual is part of a bartering system where severe crimes can be reduced to lesser crimes simply upon admission of guilt. This is because if one were to go to trial, he or she just might completely get away with the crime committed!

Know that these tactics do not exist in the ultimate court of God. There is no finagling or exploiting the due process of God's law. Not only is it absolute, it is just, and it is right. We don't prepare for such a supreme judge by practicing law the way we do – there are just too many loopholes and bias.

God is quite impartial. Every man and woman will be judged based on his or her faith in His Truth, the life lived based on exactly what was provided to the individual and then what was sown and reaped. There is no appeal. There is no retrial. Your faith and hope in God will meet an ultimate ruling. What you have been given in life such as talents, wealth, knowledge, ability, and motivation will be compared to exactly what you achieved such as generosity, faith, family, understanding, and penitence.

We find life to be too short at times and too long otherwise. It's too short when we live in the moment enjoying the fruits of God's mercy, but it is all too long when we have to pay it back or pay it forward. The shorter we think life is, the more we will just focus on ourselves – we may never even consider God once in a short life. The longer we think life is, the more apparent time we may find ourselves asking questions or trying to make sense of life itself. Despite one's perception of time, know it was all exactly as long as was needed.

Be concerned. Worry not just for yourself but for those close to you and even the strangers far from you. It is a commonality amongst us that death will surely come, and with it, a final ruling of whether or not your soul is even worth saving. The life will pass into a memory but the soul does not have to.

Within your lifetime, did you realize this? Did you realize that the world is not eternal? Neither is your body, nor your wealth or good times. Neither are your poverty or poor decisions! These were all the stepping stones required for you and you alone – the necessary requirements given to break down your pride, break down your spirit, and build you anew.

Did you accomplish this rebuilding of yourself? Did your temporary life validate the soul that you will offer up to God upon death? Or will you squander the signs? Will you squander the joys? Will you squander the tests? Do you plan to squander your entire life and from it not once look around and think how much greater than you it all is? Well?

Well, then the just judgment will be passed.

It's a hard reality in which we live today. Satan has done a good job making sure the worldly view is just as significant as any religious view. Look at all the advancements we take for granted and directly attribute it all to ourselves. The judgment of our death and life will be based on what has been provided and what we did with it. I find this to be a scary realization because we basically have everything in the world at our disposal! Communications, video, internet, a world instantaneously accessible to most. An abundance of commodities and resources, paper, metals, an infrastructure that keeps expanding even when expansion appears impossible. Even electricity – I can read at night now!

Every single necessity to find God is available to us 24/7. What have we done with that constant accessibility? Shopping? Games? Pornography? You may have finished your degree online but did you once imagine to look into what this whole religion thing is about? Did you forget to research the ancient civilizations and history of humanity? Who has time for that old junk – I have a term paper due. Who has time to worry about Truth – there are only three hours left on this Amazon sale. Who has time to find ways of saving a soul – I'm too busy burning through my entire life as fast as I can so that I never even have the chance!

Be concerned. Life here on Earth is too short and after generations of technology yielding efficient production and efficient access to information, it's getting even shorter. We are finding that we can fill our time so easily with anything, but that's not the purpose of life. We were meant to find God and His Church, not regress to an ancestry of apes or find faith in the newest technological patent.

We can fill our lives with every idolatrous, selfish, and Satanic product this world has to offer and, in that time, find just one moment for God to have a chance of salvation. That's the true power of God's mercy, but it's more popular not to consider God anymore. We don't want to spend time searching the internet for philosophical treatises, theological debates, or even what it means to be a real Christian – we'd rather watch cat videos and people setting world records.

This is the final confrontation we must face today in our lives – the complete and literally full access to righteous, holy, and religious doctrines and truths matched by our completely misguided and apathetic attitude to taking advantage of it. When you have to answer for your ignorance of holy things, of religious teaching, of God and His Church, how can you deny that you could have learned? You had ample access to every single facet of the Mind and Body of Christ – the scripture, the prophecies, the traditions, the sacraments, the truth – and you wasted it on cat videos?!

Where is the line drawn for those who wasted a life given and for those who spent even one day considering spiritual truths? Perhaps the sciences have captivated many of us so fully because they not only are empirical enough to believe but they also provide comfort and ease to our lives. Why doesn't the spiritual or religious life captivate just as many individuals? Because it's hard. It's demanding. There is no immediate sense of progress, relief, or reward, just a tremendous amount of hardship, self-reflection, utter humility, and mortification of the soul.

The stage is set for both practices of life – the physical and scientific as well as the spiritual and religious. How deeply we delve into either side will have a direct impact on our spiritual growth.

Did you find the natural order and law of things so compelling that your life was spent understanding and harnessing them? Did this knowledge expose you to such intense pride that a clouded realization of the very laws being studied emerged? So, you understand chemistry, calculus, and physics, and you're even theorizing about what could have been or what might be through quantum theorems. So, you gazed up at the stars and suddenly everything makes sense to you? Did you fashion the idea that none of it is attributed to you, or to your professors, or even to the founders of those equations and theories? Have you concluded that you are the observer in every quantifiable reaction and the audience of every recorded phenomena? You manipulate that which is already present. You split the very fabric of our reality. And now you really believe you know truth?

I don't doubt that you would excel superiorly in the standardized, man-made, education system – but the world is God's classroom. Did you spend more than a decade perfecting your manipulation of the human body but forget to acknowledge its true designer? Do not fall victim to the deception knowledge can have on your mind and reasoning. Approach the sciences with humility and you will never find yourself a contributor in anything but the immense puzzle of the Creator's divine mind and intellect. This humble stance is truly the beauty of the sciences.

If you've lived this life desperately searching for answers and equations that will solve the world's problems, then surely at least once you have felt that this task is so much greater than any one person. Yet, you expect it of yourself – demand it even. But the answer to the world's issues isn't A or B nor how much sustainable energy can be transferred through a vacuum. The answer was and is that which made any of this effort worth a damn – God.

The teacher gave us the answer to the test right from the beginning. Is that cheating? Maybe it's the greatest mercy ever bestowed upon any student of this world. But just because the answer was given prior to the test doesn't mean you won't have to understand it. If you have spent your life – instead of purely seeking physical knowledge – seeking a proper spiritual foundation, then you are already ahead of the class. Here I will state my clear bias towards spirituality and religion over physical sciences in two reasons.

Firstly, I myself started in the sciences and mathematics and it yielded as much as I put into it. I cannot and never will deny the utility, the passion, and the profound attention to detail that comes from technological and scientific advancement. However, if this is the only foundation of one's life, then that foundation is severely misguided and solely limited to that which you know – which in the sum of all things is so little.

Secondly, our lives will end and so will this physicality with which it comes. Our bodies, our world, our perceptions of the universe will eventually cease being what they are today. If this doesn't spark your curiosity of the spiritual and unseen nature of things, then what will? The perpetuity of our being is beyond the senses and the physical sciences will never be able to quantify such a truth. Do not believe there ought not be more than physicality just because you fail to sense it.

For that's the test after all – a test of faith. No equation will simply describe the sheer complexity of one's own faith or even what is required to build that faith. Thus, they who focus on the divine, the spiritual, and the religious but perhaps still falter in word, concept, or formula, are already ahead of those who expect to find all answers in physicality. They who see the futility in physicality and continue to search for that which is intangible will one day find what they seek – it requires faith and so much prayer.

How much knowledge, capability, grace, and hope has been provided to so many individuals who still manage to fail God's classroom? The prideful scientist has been blessed with such a mind to grasp and convey so much of the world, but this mind should have realized the faulty logic in believing that knowing anything means having ultimate understanding of it. The slothful and pious mind has been blessed with the acknowledgement of spirit and God yet failed to find the relationship between both.

That which is accessible today allows for any path of life that one desires to be much easier than in previous times – this is the danger at hand. Any one of us can embark on the life we believe to be right, proper, and fulfilling, yet still fail the final test.

Be concerned. Be humble. Recognize that even when you've reached a relative apex or plateau that there is still so much room for advancement that you should never cease trying to complete yourself as a human. There is no such reality that grants you a passing score on God's final test that includes complacency, stagnation, procrastination, or a refusal to progress. We each handle ourselves according to what we think our capabilities are but also according to what we are comfortable in presently confronting. Don't let this innate sufficiency hold you back.

Judgment may be final, but the road to salvation seems unending. We as humans should cope with falling short of our true potential. It is only by the mercy and grace of God that we will acquire what we spiritually need to prepare. God is so great and loving that He will provide every single thing you need to complete yourself – physically, mentally, and spiritually. This is not a one-way transfer though – you must meet God half way by means of your free will. You must pray and place petition for everything you are lacking as well as pray for God's grace, mercy, and forgiveness of sin.

The truth of judgment is terrifying not because of apocalyptic descriptions and imagery but because of its finality. View yourself in that time as the final product of all your efforts and trust in His Truth. View it as the last chance to convince the Teacher that you actually learned something. View it as the last gift you can provide God as a true token of gratitude for having allowed anything at all.

It is most merciful to provide the answers to salvation, but it is most studious to fully embrace and understand the answers provided.

A foundation of spiritual belief, faith, and knowledge will assist in the many tests that will be given throughout one's life. Physical suffering, mental anguish, spiritual penitence – these all require a foundational theory and understanding to fully appreciate the roles they play in shaping each of us spiritually.

Nothing thrown at an individual is without purpose, whether a test of faith or a test of resiliency. When confronted with adversity, the one quick to abandon notions of God and faith will mercifully be provided even more opportunities to discover such faith – most likely through further hardship and tests of the heart and soul. To the one quick to latch onto God's love and mercy shall be provided more opportunity to experience it here in this life. And even then, the tests will still come. The soul doesn't become forged and reforged overnight – it is an eternal process that just begins here in our physical lives.

Imagine how much wealth of understanding, faith, and trust in God can develop if an entire lifetime is submitted to the will of God, let alone what can be gained in the perceivable span of eternity! Even if the answers have been given – that God's will is supreme and His love and mercy are what will bring us to salvation upon our death or on the day of judgment – there is still a free will binding us to actively seek this understanding and accept it.

Mercy is not just the revelation of divine knowledge – mercy is the permittance of time to even attempt grasping such understanding. Lord have mercy, grant us peace. Lord have mercy, grant us time! There is no peace for the penitent soul who fervently and ceaselessly desires to love God and profess their sinful nature, which always falls short of the glory of God. Similarly, there is no peace for the truly impenitent soul who has abandoned faith and clung to the views and desires of this world. Two totally distant points on the spectrum of sanctity, yet both found God's love and mercy. One is given the love to grant and hear prayers as well as the mercy to grant time to save souls. The other is given the love that grants a chance of redemption as well as the mercy to keep his or her soul until death.

These lives we live are a composite amalgamation of every physical and worldly influence passed on by preceding generations. Physically, we are the product of the world. Spiritually, we can find truth and reattach ourselves to the very love and mercy that allows us to continue existing. God's mercy is so great that it continues to pour out over all the world despite our wasting of so much time – time spent forgetting who He is, who we even are, and what truly matters in our lives. If we spent as much time advancing and maturing our spirit as we did trying to advance our physical appearance and status, well, there would be so many more saints and so much more true faith in the world.

God's mercy will grant you exactly what is needed to find Him – now and upon the final days. Don't squander that which you find to be grace or a test, for how much time remains is unknown. Use this sense of urgency to cultivate a sense of action within yourself spiritually. Pray for the Holy Spirit to grant you the many graces of God and especially that of virtue, wisdom, counsel, and fear of the Lord. Everyone has a little bit of fear of their teachers – they control the very outcome of your efforts. Have the greatest fear in the greatest Teacher – it just may prove to be enough to find the remaining components of a soul worth saving.

POEMS OF FAITH

Daily Prayer

I heard gunshots today.

I wasn't scared,

I even poked my head out the window to see the occasion.

Across the street was our neighbor, he was holding his little daughter.

She had definitely been shot.

To my left I saw a group of four just walking, not even running, away.

One life stolen, one soul lifted.

All at the price of four souls.

Now I must make amends for those four lost souls, for I am a witness.

I will pray for them and maybe they will change.

But for me, I am still ever the same.

JOSEPH LEWIS

The Best Farmer I Know

My father was a hardworking man

Strict, orderly, rising early to beat the sun to the crops

But stubborn, oh so stubborn

He would insist the taxes were too high on his yield and always forgo the assistance of others because he knew he knew best the matter of things

But these persistent banters I would overlook, for he taught me well the way of the land and together we made a success of our work

He entrusted me to never give up the harvest and to pass it on to my children,

To immortalize the traditions of a proud and assured man

Thus, when it came time for me to place him into the ground for which he had given everything, I knew it would be my duty to ceaselessly serve his honor.

To my despair, and most certainly to his disappointment, as time passed, I found our land to become less and less fruitful,

Of which I could not make any sense

I tilled just as my father had done, fertilized just as he had done, eradicated the pests and weeds that my father fought his entire life, all just as he had done

Instead of inheriting an abundance of reaped rewards, I slowly watched this land wither away without the care of its previous caretaker

It was as if the spirit of my father was culling the last remnants of his work that he may keep them eternally, for this land was becoming barren beyond what I could reason

Ultimately, I was forced to remove myself from that land; he was right, the taxes were crippling and it seemed no one could tend to his beloved crops other than he

Prior to departing, I decided to plant a tree to commemorate my father

Among that wasteland of memories, I struck the Earth with a shovel and planted the last seed that would ever be given to that land,

If anything should grow there it ought to be a remembrance.

Years and many more years later, I became stricken with a sickness that would claim my own life; soon I believed, I would get to see my father again

I visited that old farmland of ours which had evolved into a peaceful community of new families, new memories, and new futures

Still, though, it was noticed the lack of any foliage or bushes

Except, to my pleasant surprise, for one prominently proud tree standing just slightly above the houses

Adjacent to that legacy of a forgotten farmer stood a church even just slightly taller than the tree, right in the heart of that community.

The irony.

The Face

When I look at the world, I cringe.

I see a realm depicting natural beauty

It's a home that we've never built but hold dear to our hearts

Sanctuary for the body and tantalizing picturesque landscapes for the mind.

But when I look at the face of another

I, too, see such natural beauty

With welcoming arms and smiles, "please come in, make yourself at home,

I will talk to you about pleasant stories and a history that you have never seen but can imagine."

And when I am tucked into bed, I begin to feel the dread

Even here in an old friend's home, I am a viable candidate

A naïve and unsuspecting victim of the cruel intentions hidden behind the gentle gaze of crystalline eyes and the glinting gems of sharpened fangs just recently chiseled for friendly banter.

When I look at your face, I assume.

I assume there is a gentle heart and a warm soul

That you mean no harm and could do no harm

But we both have seen where the presumption of kindness has led innocence,

Countless bones and innumerable vials of blood stashed away in this home of ours

You invited me into your home, and luckily, I found the skeletons in the closet before it was inevitable that I become one

And still, we share a common home even beyond the walls of your own

Beyond the confines of your own mind, your own will, your own body

We're both kept safe within the walls of Bluebeard's castle we call the world.

Its surreal serenity is the open invitation to become one with it, now and ever

An alluring affirmation that this home is and always will be your home, "Do not look elsewhere, you'd only be wasting your time!"

A sinister seduction that seizes your senses and holds faith for ransom

When I look right into the face of the world, it looks back at me.

With that distorted and twisted face aged by millenniums of captivating the curiosity of the curious and enchanting the ethereal dreams of the dreamers

Its eyes no longer the crystalline ponds of purity and respite but instead become the surreptitious cesspools of wasted souls

And that beaming smile of a promised land has become a gaping cavern stretching into the deepest, darkest intentions covered by a veil of deceit.

Yes, when I look at the world, I cringe.

For I know its secret,

It's a secret that remains hidden the longer you look right at it, but becomes so much clearer once you turn away.

It is Finished (John 19:30 NSRV)

Having but just found my own soul,

I ask how it can be sanctified and pleasing to God

To which is answered through trials and suffering.

Naturally I ask what is the greatest trial and suffering that I may enact

To which is answered complete detachment and submission to the will of God.

With each answer, I formulate more questions, to this last I now have two more.

How am I certain of complete detachment?

To which is answered when you have removed all inclination towards pleasing the world and gaining its things.

And how can I be certain of complete submission to the will of God?

To which is answered when you deny your own satisfaction in place of God's you are fulfilling more than your own will.

I shan't overlook any possibility of true suffering, would not sacrifice be pleasing to the will of God?

To which is answered sacrifice with the intention of glorifying God is truly pleasing.

Well, I am a rational creature, is not the greatest sacrifice I may offer that of my own life?

To which is answered giving all for the glory of God definitely means giving up even the life given.

Wouldst thou bless those even whom haven't given a life entirely to the will of God?

To which is answered in their time of need the grace and mercy of God will be shown clearly.

But my fears of a blind people cause me to desire reconciling their fault on their account,

Is not the truest sacrifice one can give the death of this physical life?

To which is answered those whom have been persecuted and martyred for the glory of God are truly blessed.

Then no longer have I any questions; I declare that I am willing to die for the preservation of even the lost souls.

To which I still receive an answer.

I already have.

The Voyage

Unfathomable is the mercy that awaits.

Within the unquenchable flames of purification does the sin finally depart from the sinner

Will it bring about pain and misery?

Most undoubtedly,

But not for the correlated reasons we find physical agony so disconcerting

No, the spiritual agony wrought by the purgative flame does not touch the flesh or the senses,

It is from deep within that the hurt soul will find its own incineration

Hopefully here within a lifetime.

For the mercy bestowed upon the sinner is not one of temporary embrace

Eternal desire to ascend the spirit and call it back home,

Unstained and pure,

Is a mercy that warrants the willful participant in one's own cleansing.

How disheartened is the mother who watches her child fall from her?

Falling into the chaotic chasms of concupiscence,

Falling into the grasp of another life, one that she did not bear.

Stained by sin,

Impure from impurity,

But would not that same mother wipe the face of her child who returned home?

In order for her to see the face of that beloved child again

She would wipe away the mud and dirt,

Wipe away the blood and tears,

Just to see the face she once knew.

She sits at home wanting, loving, and praying for that day to come.

For it won't be her own accord that stirs the penitence in even her own child,

First the reluctance must be defeated.

The sinful must find their own will in a life so willing to keep it subdued

Repentance is not just the admission of guilt and shame,

It is a complete change in direction

Freeing our vessel from mirky waters so it may embark on the true journey from the dunghill toward the divine.

Fathomless depths of merciful waters is the final destination our compass leads us.

Yet opposing gusts cause swaying from the straight route

The tempestuous temptation tries to deliver us to calm waters.

Our ship slows to a halt.

Why is the water here so still?

So dead?

It is in these complacent waters that the crew will be forgotten in the graveyard of lost ships.

For it is not through calm water we find mercy,

But through the calamity of cleansing,

And the burning away of the anchor keeping us from going home.

What Man can Deny Jesus?

Weren't we all children once?

Nurtured by our mother, hardened by our father

Lest you had no mother,

Then hopefully you found compassion in your father's rule

Lest you had no father,

Then you had to find strength in your mother's love

Lest you were orphaned,

Oh, how cruel a world can be to a child who knows not origin.

Yet, collectively we were all children

Teething through tears,

Bearing growing pains of brittle bones and brittle hearts.

Our bodies age and yield proof that no longer are we children.

But what is the yolk that remains inside our ripened shell?

What man can deny Jesus?

He is the man who externalizes his worth and fails to crack his ego.

He finds comfort in the mirror seeing how age has treated him well

Seeing the superficial standards to which he has lived.

The man who denies Christ is a man who denies the child within.

He would be ashamed should anyone look inside and find that dead child,

The child who longed to find peace in salvation and hope in another life.

A lost child.

He buried the boy inside himself long ago

And as he has grown old with the world, he shall die with the world.

No man can deny Christ,

Lest he has already killed the child inside himself.

Infanticide is the sin of this man,

For he has killed yet another child of God.

My Will be Done

I had the choice to be a priest.

Commit everything to the faith and hope of Jesus

His church, His people, His sinners and His saints

But how could the righteous connect with such blatant societal rejections of God?

So therefore,

I made the choice to be a drunk.

Dedicated my time to understanding myself

My world, my friends, my gals and my bottles

But how could the willingly sinful connect with the necessity of good citizens?

So then,

I made the choice to be a medley of social, ethical, and moral traits.

Imitated the body of perfection that others seek

Their expectations, their views, no longer my own volition or desire

But how can a puppet string the corporal and spiritual attitudes together flawlessly?

So now,

I have made the choice to end it all.

Expedite the inevitable future of a life given

A fate, a choice, permanent and decisive

But how can the dead affect what had been the original intent?

At least then I would have been a damned priest...

SUGGESTED MATERIAL

Paradise Lost – John Milton
The Life of Christ – Fulton Sheen
The Consolation of Philosophy – Boethius
Find God's Will For You – St. Francis de Sales
Dark Night of the Soul – St. John of the Cross
Deliverance Prayers – Fr. Chad Ripperger, PhD
The Mystical City of God – Venerable Mary of Agreda
The Practice of the Presence of God – Brother Lawrence

9 781489 735492